Aggression in the Workplace
Preventing and Managing High-Risk Behavior

---

*A crisis management approach
to threats of violence and aggressive behavior
in the workplace*

Marc McElhaney, Ph.D.
Critical Response Associates

authorHOUSE™

*1663 LIBERTY DRIVE, SUITE 200
BLOOMINGTON, INDIANA 47403
(800) 839-8640
WWW.AUTHORHOUSE.COM*

First published by AuthorHouse 10/14/04

ISBN: 1-4184-6195-4 (sc)
ISBN: 1-4184-6196-2 (dj)

Library of Congress Control Number: 2004095922

Printed in the United States of America
Bloomington, Indiana

This book is printed on acid-free paper.

To the memory of Jennie and Howard McElhaney,
a creative team if there ever was one.

About the Author

Dr. Marc McElhaney serves as director of Critical Response Associates and the President of its parent organization, the Centers for Dispute Resolution, LLC. He received his Ph.D. in clinical and community psychology from the University of South Florida, and currently resides in Atlanta, Georgia.

As a consulting psychologist and certified mediator, Dr. McElhaney works exclusively in the areas of threat assessment, critical incident management, and conflict resolution. Since 1977, he has consulted with hundreds of organizations (typically large corporations and law enforcement agencies) in regards to the assessment, management, and resolution of high-risk incidents. He has also helped schools and corporations develop workplace violence policies and crisis response programs, and currently presents workshops and training programs in the areas of workplace violence prevention, conflict resolution, and crisis management.

The author is an active member of several professional organizations, including the American Psychological Association, the Association of Threat Assessment Professionals, the Association for Conflict Resolution, the American Society for Industrial Security, Psychologists for Social Responsibility, the Society for Human Resource Management, and the National Register of Health Care Providers in Psychology.

Dr. McElhaney welcomes your comments and inquiries. The reader is welcome to contact him toll free at 1-888-584-4200 or by e-mail at mmcelhan@aol.com. More information about his work is available at www.cdresolve.com.

Preface

Mark Twain once said that the universal symbol of the human race should be a man (or woman) dragging an ax, because "everyone has one to grind."

By definition, every author's book imports his or her agenda or perhaps grinds his or her ax—and mine is no different. One's agenda is influenced by the idiosyncratic perspective from which each of us surveys the procession of events in our lives.

This book is certainly a product of my perspective and carries my agenda, based on what I do for a living. It is both enhanced and limited by my particular angle of view. I hope that it offers something of what I have learned as a consulting psychologist in the general area of crisis and conflict management.

The focus of this book is restricted to the phenomenon of aggressive and related high-risk behaviors that occur within organizations. My purpose is very simply to present: 1) my experience and perspective; 2) the conclusions that I have gleaned from those experiences, and finally; 3) a set of guidelines that I recommend to address this issue, based on those conclusions.

The source of this experience has evolved from my role as a consultant to organizations, typically corporations. Our services are usually requested when an organization is confronted with an individual or a situation that may potentially be at risk of becoming violent, or who is otherwise significantly disruptive.

Sometimes a threat has been made, or there exists behavior that is at the least considered threatening by others. It may be behavior that is severely disruptive to the company's normal operations, or is for some reason not controllable within the company's usual internal procedures. There is often a question about the individual's mental status, and there is always uncertainty about his or her potential for harm. Sometimes, these concerns are more ambiguous and less definable, based on disturbingly aberrant or socially inappropriate acts.

Our initial task is to assess the risk that this individual or situation presents, and to advise the company in regards to both the immediate steps and the overall process that will eventually facilitate a safe resolution. Much of the time, this also includes an engagement with the subject, as part of both the assessment and management process. This will sometimes evolve into an intervention that would generally fall under the heading of crisis negotiation, which more often than not involves defusing and managing someone who is hostile and emotionally destabilized.

Once the immediate safety concerns are successfully resolved, but before we close the case, we want to ensure that we have also addressed any residual long-term issues. The goal is to anticipate and identify any possible long-term risks, and to enact procedures that will insulate all the involved parties to whatever degree is possible. We do not want anyone to feel that they must forever be looking over their shoulder.

Whenever possible, we accomplish that by attempting to eventually develop "win-win" solutions, to utilize a perhaps overused but very significant phrase. Our assessment and management of critical incidents always includes a focus on the needs and primary interests of those involved. A critical element of the ultimate goal is to ensure that the subjects of concern walk away with a belief that they were heard, and that their concerns were addressed in a fair and good faith manner—and we have been generally able to accomplish that. We have found this to constitute a critical ingredient in our ability to manage these risks of violence over the long haul.

In the course of my work, I have had the opportunity and the luxury of hindsight. I have been able to review the unfolding of the events that have led to scenarios where people suddenly felt that their lives were threatened. I have been able to review what works and what does not.

This book is written not because I have it all figured out, but because I thought I might have just enough that would be worth sharing. My intent and hope is that this will serve more as a "guidebook" for those who manage at different levels of an organization, as opposed to serving as a philosophical or academic discourse. As worthy as academic texts are, I wanted to write this as a guide that will be useful and applicable in "real life."

Much of this is derived from my and my associates' experiences, and may not all be supported by any kind of rigorous scientific research. Some concepts you will hopefully recognize in other works, as we—the practitioners in this area—all seem to be stumbling on the same general ideas and principles, although our individual approaches may differ.

Fields such as threat assessment, crisis negotiation and dispute resolution are all rather nascent fields of study, and are often practiced as both art and science. However, concepts are emerging from these and other areas, that represent exciting new possibilities and which provide real, practical value.

As always, I would like to acknowledge those who have made this possible—those who have helped to provide all those learning experiences and who perhaps more importantly, have helped make this learning process an enjoyable one. This I find to be an almost impossible task, as I—like everyone—cannot always determine when and where certain seeds were planted, and I want to avoid sounding like an award winner who is intent on thanking the universe. Most of those in my extended universe know who they are, and I am deeply appreciative.

That being said, I would like to specifically mention those colleagues from various disciplines with whom I have shared many experiences in the course of this rather intense work in the management of workplace violence—and without question, this is *always* a team effort. I would like to particularly mention Todd Conklin, Michael Corcoran, Phil Cox, Leslie Davis, Michael Hardman, Rosalind Jackson, John Manelos, Bill McGrath, Chad Shultz, Tony Stone, and Steve White. Finally and most importantly, my wife Debra, and my children Amie and Brian, for their love and support.

Marc McElhaney, Ph.D.
September 1, 2004

Table of Contents

Introduction Aggression and Violence at Work: *Is it really that bad?* 1

Chapter 1   The Importance of Preparation and Prevention..7
- Aggression vs. Violence: *Defining Our Terms* 7
- The Costs of Workplace Violence 10
- The Organizations's Obligations...............................12
- Is Workplace Violence Preventable? 16
- When an Employee "Snaps"....................................17
- The Issue of Denial and Avoidance 19
- Violence as a Process...20

Chapter 2   Who Commits Workplace Violence: *Identifying the At-Risk Employee* 23
- "The Profile"...23
- So, Do We Have a Profile or Not?............................26
- Predicting Violence: *The Dynamics of Risk Assessment* 27
- Threat Assessment as a Specialized Process 28
- The Process of Threat Assessment: *An Overview* 28
- The Individual: *Static Factors* 30
- The Effect of Stress: *Emotional Aspects*...................35
- Situational Factors 39
- Critical Elements in Threat Communications 41
- Warning Signs 42
- Common Antecedents of Workplace Violence 43

Chapter 3   Common Errors and Oversights *(What You Do Not Want to Hear)* 47

- *"He just kind of snapped."* 48
- *"How did we let this thing get this far?"* 49
- *"Why did we hire this guy in the first place?"* 50
- *"We don't have anything in the file."* 51
- *"We can always just call the police."* 53
- *"We referred him to an EAP."* 54
- *"We did not want to make him angry."* 56
- *"We just didn't take him seriously."* 57
- *"That's just the way he/she is."* 58
- *"She just hasn't been herself lately."* 59
- *"We just want to get rid of him."* 60
- *"This guy just gives me the creeps."* 62
- *"It won't do any good to report it."* 63
- *"I don't want to get in trouble."* 63
- *"I didn't know who to call."* 64
- *"She said that she was afraid of him."* 65
- *"We don't have those kind of problems here."* 66

Chapter 4   Preventing Workplace Violence: *A Ten-Step Solution* 69

- Pre-Employment Screening...70
- The Workplace Violence Policy 74
- Promoting Employee Involvement.............................79
- Employee Training Programs 80
- A Threat Response Plan 83
- Grievance, Disciplinary, and Termination Processes ..84
- Employee Assistance Programs 87
- Outplacement Services..88

- Training Supervisory & Conflict Resolution Skills 89
- Utilizing Outside Resources 91

Chapter 5   Responding to a Threat: *An Overview of the*
Assessment and Management Process..............................93
- What Constitutes a "Threat?" 93
- The Threat Response Team 96
- Initiating the Threat Response Process......................98
- The Subject Interview..106
- Response Strategies 109
- Return-to-Work Decisions......................................112
- Monitoring and Follow-up 114
- The Threat Assessment Professional 115
- The ADA and Other Legal Concerns......................117

Chapter 6   Safe Terminations 123
- The Crisis of Job Loss..123
- Separating High-Risk Employees 125
- Threat Assessment at Termination 138
- The Logistics of the Termination Process................142

Chapter 7   Defusing Angry Employees: *A Manager's Guide to*
Crisis & Conflict Resolution...149
- The Principles of Crisis/Conflict Negotiation 150
- The Steps in Conflict Resolution 151
- The Win-Win Solution 152
- Controlling Natural Responses 153
- Techniques of De-escalation....................................155
- Needs Identification and Reframing........................163
- The Journey to Problem-Solving: *Getting to "we"* ..168

Chapter 8   Stalking and Predatory Behaviors In the Workplace..173

- Affective vs. Predatory Violence 174
- The Psychopathic Personality................................175
- The Impact of Paranoia and Delusional Thinking 178
- Stalking Behaviors...181
- Stalking and the Workplace 182
- Cyberstalking 185
- Management of Predatory and Stalking Behaviors...186

Epilogue   The Future *(if we want it)*................................193

Appendix A A Sample Workplace Violence Policy 197
Appendix B An Organizational Self-Assessment Questionnaire..203
Appendix C Violence Assessment: Interview Checklist.......211
Appendix D A Sample Return to Work Agreement.............223
Appendix E A Sample Termination Agreement 227

References... 233

Introduction

Aggression and Violence at Work
Is it really that bad?

When I first became involved in this field, I carried a presumption that much of the publicity about the increased violence and danger in our society (and in our workplace in particular) was at least to some degree a product of media attention. I assumed that like many of our social "maladies of the day," the proverbial grain of truth lay buried under a great deal of media-driven sensationalism. After all, hardly a week goes by that we are not subjected to some tragic account of the "disgruntled" employee who has decided to randomly inflict a horrific toll in his or her workplace—a toll that takes the lives of some and forever changes the lives of others.

On the other hand, it has been equally clear that considering that we are an otherwise civilized, stable, and affluent society, we have always been a comparatively violent one. That is hardly in doubt, and is well documented. The United States has one of the highest reported homicide rates in the industrialized world, a rate 10 times higher than England and 25 times higher than Spain. And based on my and others' subjective experiences, our culture appears to be becoming increasingly contentious and less "well-mannered," for lack of a better term.

The reasons for this level of violence are much debated and unfortunately so dependent on one's political, philosophical, or religious agenda, that it is difficult to maintain a reasonable discourse on the subject. Here we will take the coward's way out and not even attempt to address the question of the root causes of American violence. That is another book, and a subject that—when all is said and done—may only serve to get in our way.

Even with those assumptions, I still initially presumed that much of the actual aggression that occurred in the workplace more than likely simply consisted of the byproducts of the common conflicts that are always part and parcel of human relationships—in addition perhaps to a few well-publicized incidents at the post office.

However, after years of working as a consulting psychologist in the general area of threat assessment and what we have come to term "critical incident management," I am continually and increasingly astounded by the pervasiveness of this phenomenon, and I have come to the conclusion that it is not over-sensationalized. In fact, I believe that this phenomenon is essentially *under-reported*.

On a regular basis, my colleagues and I are privy to events that are *alarming* in terms of their potential for disastrous results—events that have the potential for explosive consequences if left unmanaged. Perhaps many of them would have resolved themselves without harm, but the costs of inaction, given the possible consequences, can be overwhelming.

The tip of the proverbial iceberg

When consulting with a company regarding a particular individual or issue, we will initially interview supervisors, human resources representatives, and other members of management, as part of the investigative or planning process. More often than not, we will discover in this process, *other* events and *other* individuals that have created a very serious (sometimes unspoken) level of concern for some of the organization's managers, but have somehow not yet risen to a critical level, sufficient to trigger an active response. By the end of the day, we often find ourselves discussing these *other* employees instead of the subject of the original referral, because they had come to actually represent an even greater level of concern.

These may be employees who have always raised a manager's anxiety, but decisions were postponed or avoided because managers either were unaware that there were available options, or perhaps preferred the delusion of "safety" that delay and avoidance offer. The discussion itself breaks through that rather normal pattern of denial, and when the tips of these icebergs are explored, we often find a situation with all the ingredients of a potentially explosive situation—a fuse waiting to be lit.

We will likewise sometimes interview the peers and coworkers of the subject employee, for the purpose of gaining additional information. In the course of these interviews, we will uncover *yet again* other employees of concern who had not come to the attention of anyone in management. These employees will inform us in no uncertain terms that while our designated employee may certainly be a problem, there are *others* who produce an even *greater* degree of fear among their coworkers. These are often individuals whom many in the workforce—even the toughest "machos" on the line—have learned to avoid, for fear of the possible consequences. Remarkably, these individuals may have been engaging in threatening behaviors for years without coming to the attention of management—even their immediate supervisors.

Finally, when we present our training workshops on the issue of workplace violence, there is inevitably a waiting group of administrative, human resources, and/or security managers after the presentation, anxious to discuss ongoing incidents of concern, sometimes with an urgent request for consultation that "can't wait."

This rather consistent pattern underscores not only the prevalence of the problem, but also the relative lack of known options. The result is that little or no action has been taken to address cases that were literally waiting in the wings, postponed for fear of the possible consequences. These managers have often referred to themselves as sitting on "powder kegs," not knowing how to respond, or if a response in itself may set off a destructive series of consequences.

The facts and figures

The research consistently appears to support the subjective experiences mentioned above. While violence in our society as a whole seems to have stabilized (a relatively small degree of consolation), violence in the workplace is apparently rising at a comparatively rapid pace. The workplace has become our forum for expressing our frustrations, whether these are related to our jobs or not—and like it or not.

I do not intend to bore you with multiple statistics, as I think that these can be not only redundant but often are used to simply alarm. I will mention a few that I believe exemplify and confirm the issue that is before us.

Regarding the most serious result of workplace aggression, it is notable that in the United States, *homicide* is the number two cause of workplace death for men (behind motor vehicle accidents) and number one for women.[1] Homicide is however, but one manifestation (albeit the most serious), and represents a relatively small percentage of the results of workplace violence. Homicides receive more news coverage, but the prevalence and results of the full range of workplace aggression are far more extensive and costly.

In a study conducted by the Northwestern National Life Insurance Institute for Occupational Safety and Health, *one of four* workers were harassed, threatened, or attacked on the job in a *one-year period*. As a result of those incidences, 88% of the workers say that they were *psychologically affected,* 62% report that their *work was disrupted,* 23% were *physically injured* or sick. Only 7% reported no negative effect![2]

A survey by the Society for Human Resource Management (SHRM), found that *one third* of the workplaces experienced a violent incident in the *prior three years*.[3] In a follow-up survey three years later, they found that the problem had escalated, with fully *one half* of the HR managers reporting at least one incident in the three years since the prior survey.[4]

All that being said, I believe this phenomenon to represent an increasingly critical problem within our society, and this view is reinforced every day. The Centers for Disease Control has recently dubbed workplace violence an "epidemic" problem, such that it has become an issue that is being increasingly addressed by regulatory and legal bodies, as will be discussed in the following chapter.

Although "going postal" has perhaps become a permanent part of our vocabulary, this is not simply a problem at the post office. While the U.S. Postal Service may have had its problems, we have found that workplace violence is not restricted to types of business or positions or roles within the organization. Everyone is now vulnerable. There is also an assumption often that this is a primarily "blue collar" problem, but my experience argues otherwise. Further, it appears to be becoming more than just an American phenomenon (Leather et al, 1999). For whatever reason (and there are probably many), aggressive behavior and threats of violence in the workplace are becoming increasingly so pervasive that events which would dominate the headlines nationwide just a few years ago are now more often relegated to the back pages of our local newspapers.

Endnotes

[1] National Institute for Occupational Safety and Health (NIOSH), as cited in Labig (1995).

[2] "Fear and Violence in the Workplace," Northwestern National Life Insurance Survey (Employee Benefits Division), Minneapolis, October 1993.

[3] "Violence in the Workplace Survey Results," Society for Human Resource Management, December 1993.

[4] "Workplace Violence," Society for Human Resource Management, Alexandria, VA, June 1996. See also "Workplace Violence Threats Common, SHRM Finds," *Individual Employment Rights,* July 2, 1996.

Chapter 1

The Importance of
Preparation and Prevention

Aggression vs. Violence
Defining Our Terms

In discussing the issue of "workplace violence," it is important to spend a moment commenting on the terms that are utilized in this book. This has become a critical issue because to some extent, the understanding of what is or is not "violence" (which is the most utilized term in the literature) is in itself partially responsible for some of the more common mistakes that are committed in this area, especially those that involve negligence.

The reader will note that these two terms, aggression and violence, are used almost interchangeably in this book. However, "aggression" (and not "violence") was chosen as the operative word in the title, for an intended reason. When we speak of "workplace violence," there appears to be a tendency for many to assume a scenario wherein a camouflaged, disgruntled psychopath with a wild-eyed stare enters the workplace spraying bullets from his AK-47 into his fleeing coworkers. Not that this does not occur, but this represents a small fraction of what most of those in this field consider to constitute violence.

Interestingly, it is for this reason that the topic is often ignored or the problems overlooked, because after all, "We don't have people like that around here," which is a frequent comment that underlies the stereotype that many have of the typical violent perpetrator. To some extent, if we review dictionary definitions, this may not be an inaccurate presumption. We find that the word "violence" generally does indeed imply a physical use of force that is notable in its *"extreme"* destructiveness, and the word "violent" is sometimes used to describe any kind of extreme phenomenon.

While these two terms will continue to be used together or interchangeably, the focus of this book is on the general behavior of *"aggression,"* which generally implies a *"hostile or threatening act,"* according to most definitions. It does not have to be a physical act, nor does it have to represent the extreme end of the continuum. While we may refer to the phenomenon of "workplace violence," we must focus our attention on *all* acts of "aggression."

Violence and aggression come in many varied forms, with a variety of consequences. And as we will see later, it does not come often from the "profile" or stereotype that many may envision. It generally does not resemble what we see on television, nor does it play out the way that we may have imagined. For that reason, it can catch us off guard and unprepared.

We will be discussing in this volume workplace violence as a concept that focuses on the *process* by which it occurs, that relies on aggressive behaviors. The reader will not be provided with much in the way of "cookbooks" or profiles, as the road to violence can take many forms, and those who commit violence can be as different from each other as they are from our stereotypic profiles. The danger of profiles, as will later be discussed, serves often to restrict our attention, and it is this *attention* that is the most necessary and critical ingredient in the process of preventing this violence from occurring in the first place.

Violence and aggression are both defined here as *any kind of conduct that is intimidating, hostile, offensive, or threatening.*

This can occur through words, actions, or physical contact. "Actions" in turn can take a variety of forms, from vandalism to hostile e-mails to "cyberstalking," which often are precursors to physical assault. These words connote by definition, a destructive quality, without positive consequences.

Behavior whose aim is to abuse or harass others is an aggressive or a violent act, with intent to harm. Its intent may be actually to cause psychological harm, which can be more devastating to the individual and the organization over the long term. Emotionally abusive behavior may include bullying, verbal humiliation, and public ridicule, but may also be represented by even more passive-aggressive forms, such as spreading rumors, withholding critical information, harassing phone calls, etc.

A broad definition of workplace violence is adopted here for several reasons, but primarily because its intent is to harm others. There is a presumption here that an organization's primary goal is to protect its employees, its customers, and the general public from malicious harm in *all* of its various forms

Additionally, once an employee or anyone else engages in activity to harm others, and if this behavior does not result in negative consequences, then it is assumed consciously or not that this is somehow permissible behavior. This aggression is therefore reinforced, such that it can (and often does) escalate. The employee who inflicts serious harm on other employees does indeed often have a history of engaging in other kinds of aggressive actions, which may not always include physical violence.

Sometimes, the subject's presentation has been such that it has created a climate of fear. The employee may be engaging in a variety of behaviors that are sustained, with the intent of (or at least resulting in) intimidation. These can be physical behaviors such as glaring menacingly, brushing up against others, or getting "too close for comfort" in their arguments, or it can be represented by a range of provocative comments such as alluding to their use of weapons, making references to their associations with hate groups, or even simply speaking in a tone that is considered "ominous" by others. They may engage in volatile and erratic behaviors that almost always leave others on edge, never knowing how the subject may react. These and numerous other (sometimes subtle) behaviors have the effect of relaying a message to others: *"You may not be safe around me ... but you never know."* In our definition, this *creation of fear in others can in itself represent a form of violence.*

We have witnessed numerous incidents of aggressive behaviors that would be considered far less serious or dramatic than the stereotypic bullet-spraying assailant, but which nonetheless impacted the workplace greatly. Understanding the broad nature of violence and aggression (regardless of which term we use) with its many forms and antecedents is a critical ingredient in being able to prevent its destructive consequences.

The Costs of Workplace Violence

To state that the price of not addressing this phenomenon can be *enormous* may appear to be rather obvious, but the consequences are far more wide-ranging than is often realized.

There should of course be little need to discuss the consequences of physical injury and even death. An individual with a lethal weapon can destroy so much in just a matter of seconds, sometimes hinged on a decisive point of action (or inaction). When reviewing past incidents of workplace violence, it is always wrenching to realize that a single decision or oversight—that would in other circumstances be deemed relatively minor—became a critical mistake, with tragic and overwhelming costs.

In the case of explosive violence, the lives of the survivors can be changed, often forever. For those who experience a traumatic event, there is a recovery period that is, more often than not, longer and more debilitating than would be anticipated. We are all desensitized to the idea and image of violence from the cinema, television, the evening news, etc., but that desensitization hardly prepares us for the trauma of real bullets. And those who have only their television experience on which to rely do not and cannot understand the emotional havoc that real trauma or near misses can wreak on the lives of those affected.

However, physical harm and death are not the most frequent or sometimes even the most negative consequences of aggressive behavior. For the affected employees, the stress of these events costs a sense of safety, undermines morale, and can erode the employees' trust in and relationship with their employer.

Traumas, in turn, produce infighting and sometimes blaming, and many employees eventually leave, as they are never able to retrieve their sense of belonging, feeling that the company has been somehow changed by the events. *Productivity* is always affected by disruptive, "high-maintenance" employees, even if there are no events that their coworkers believe are "reportable." Sometimes, good employees will eventually resign in order to avoid having to work around an abusive coworker whose behavior is somehow chronically overlooked by management.

Costs to the company also include significant *health care expenses, missed work, and worker's compensation claims.* Workplace violence causes almost a half million employees to miss 1.8 million workdays (not including sick or annual leave) each year, which translates into more than $55 million in lost wages.[1]

There are invariably *legal costs* in today's litigious environment, as companies can be sued for a variety of negligence issues, which will be discussed in the next chapter. With an average out-of-court settlement reported to be in excess of $500,000 and an average jury award at $3 million, taking actions to avoid charges of negligence would appear cost-effective.[2] The Workplace Violence Institute reports that the annual overall costs to American businesses exceed *$36 billion* for all the losses stemming from acts of workplace violence.[3]

The *company's reputation* can always be affected in today's world of instant information, as the same images are continually broadcast on the television news outlets. Larger, higher-profile organizations have difficulty escaping the media attention and the over-analysis and second-guessing that may ensue. Imagine how a corporate entity's bottom line in a competitive market is affected if they were somehow forever identified with a traumatic event that was alleged to be due to their negligence, such that "going postal" was replaced with another slogan that included the corporation's name.

Many of the organization's resources are diverted just to deal with all the direct and indirect consequences of this event. Productivity inevitably drops for all of these and other reasons, and the lifeblood of the organization is affected.

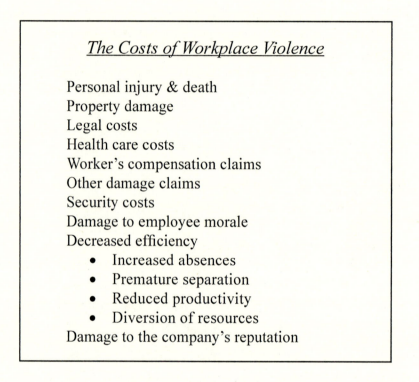

The Costs of Workplace Violence

Personal injury & death
Property damage
Legal costs
Health care costs
Worker's compensation claims
Other damage claims
Security costs
Damage to employee morale
Decreased efficiency
- Increased absences
- Premature separation
- Reduced productivity
- Diversion of resources
Damage to the company's reputation

The Organization's Obligations

It has become increasingly important for companies to prepare themselves for incidents involving workplace violence, for reasons beyond the above-mentioned costs. Legal and regulatory decisions and actions have emerged that underscore the general consensus that employers have a "duty of care" to safeguard their employees and customers.

OSHA Requirements

Beginning in 1994, the policy of the Occupational Safety and Health Administration (OSHA) has been to increasingly cite employers who failed to adequately protect their workers from acts of violence, under Section 5(a) of the OSH Act and under its "General Duty" clause. An employer has violated the law if it fails to take action to correct conditions that contribute to injuries related to workplace violence.

OSHA has issued specific guidelines regarding workplace violence in several industries, which are meant to be operable in any type of work environment. According to these guidelines, the four elements of a successful workplace violence prevention program are:

1) Management commitment and employee involvement
2) Workplace analysis
3) Hazard prevention and control
4) Training and education.

The guidelines also recommend a system of documentation that ensures that employees feel comfortable reporting potential or actual violence.

> *"Employees can be cited for violating the...Clause if there is a recognized hazard of workplace violence in their establishments and they do nothing to prevent or abate it."*
> *-OSHA 3148, 1998 (Revised)*

Legal Implications

The courts in most states have generally ruled that employers have a "duty of care" toward their employees and their customers, to take reasonable steps to prevent violence on their premises and to adequately respond to known risks.

The courts are permitting employees to bring suits under various charges of negligence, and there have been some rather dramatic and costly examples of the success of these lawsuits for the plaintiffs:

- *Negligent hiring* refers to the liability of an employer who, in the process of hiring someone, fails to reasonably obtain or consider information that would indicate that the applicant represented a risk to others.
  Example: A $26.5 million award to the estate of a patient who was beaten to death by an employee of a home health care agency. The agency failed to discover during the employee's application process that he was a six-time convicted felon. *Ward v. Boston Visiting Nursing Association,* 94-4297-H (Superior Court Suffolk Co., MA Feb 12, 1998).

- *Negligent retention* refers to an employer who retains an existing employee (or fails to take action) when the employer becomes aware (or should have become aware) of information suggesting that the employee presents a risk to other employees.
  Example: A $3.5 million dollar award against Amtrak in 1987 to a supervisor who was shot and seriously wounded by an employee whom the company failed to discipline for previous actions that indicated violent tendencies. (*Smith v. Amtrak,* 1987)[4]

- *Negligent termination* claims can occur when either an employer reacts too hastily and terminates a reportedly violent employee without exercising reasonable care in regards to their investigation of the allegation, or when the employer fails to adequately address the effect that the termination process will have on the safety of others.
  Example: A $7.2 million award against two companies that jointly managed a plant, after failing to take special precautions when terminating a potentially violent

employee. The employee shot four employees, killing three of them. *State v. Davis,* 506 S.E. 2d 455 (N.C. 1998).

- **Negligent security** refers to a failure by the employee to provide reasonable physical security for its employees and customers, to protect them from potentially foreseeable sources of harm.
  Example: A \$5.2 million award to an employee of Conner Peripherals (San Jose, CA) who was shot and permanently disabled by a former employee, whom the security guards had failed to remove from the premises, even though he was not allowed to return.[5]

- **Negligent referencing/duty to warn** refers to rulings that have stated that the employer may have a duty to warn others who are suspected to be dangerous, even future employers.
  Example: A Florida State Court judge allowed the families of office workers killed by a fellow employee to seek compensatory and punitive damages against a *former* employer of that employee, who did not disclose their concerns or evidence concerning a possible propensity for violence. Settled out of court for an undisclosed sum. *Jerner v. Allstate Insurance Co.,* No. 93-0-9472 (Florida Circuit Court, 1995).

- **Negligent training.** Some states are enacting or considering legislation that *requires* companies to develop security plans and training programs to address the issue of workplace violence. It is anticipated that this represents a growing trend.

The overall result of all this is that if a violent act or threat occurs in the workplace and the company *could have known* about it or *should have known* about it and did not respond adequately, or was not adequately prepared, then it may be determined that they bear some responsibility and liability.

The bottom line: companies that do not prepare for the possibility that violence can occur within their workplace risk potentially expensive consequences.

Is Workplace Violence Preventable?

Many in the general public appear to entertain two prevailing assumptions that are sometimes contradictory. The first is the belief that the issue of violence is not a phenomenon that we as human beings can hope to bring under complete control—that this is something that we have to accept, as part of the dark side of "human nature."

This belief assumes that we are somehow always going to have "those kind of people," and that all we can do is to respond effectively (i.e., flee or shoot) when they go on some sort of rampage. If those who invest in this belief system are asked about solutions, they generally address some kind of systemic issue (i.e. the failure of the legal system, society's moral decay, etc.) that leaves us feeling equally helpless.

The second prevailing belief is that those who commit these acts can be readily identified by some kind of single, well-defined profile, an issue that will be addressed in a later chapter. This chapter focuses on the question underlying the first belief.

As stated previously, there may be root (cultural, biological, systemic, etc.) issues that influence violence, but that's hardly helpful to a manager faced with a threat. The question here is: Can the organization prevent acts of violence within its workplace, regardless of what is occurring in the culture at large? The answer is an unequivocal <u>yes</u>!

If we have learned only two prevailing "truths" about workplace violence in our work, they are simply these:

1) Workplace violence is a serious problem (see Introduction), and
2) Workplace violence is preventable.

I will go out on this limb far enough to state that almost all workplace violence can be prevented, which will hopefully become more believable by the end of this book. In order to prevent aggression and violence, it must be assumed that there exist some kinds of antecedent events that are observable or somehow knowable.

When an Employee "Snaps"

On the initial contact, the first thing that most of us in this field invariably hear on the other end of the phone is: "We have a new situation that has just come up. Can you help us?" The communication usually describes a "new" situation that has just recently come to the manager's attention. Oftentimes, this is indeed accurate, as this is "new" in the sense that it had not been within anyone's attention prior to this triggering event. It is perceived as an event that has suddenly exploded in an otherwise uneventful day.

We also encounter accounts in the media involving apparently sudden tragic acts of violence, with the bystanders explaining how the perpetrator "just snapped." The implication, sometimes explicit, is that this was a normal, average Joe, without any history of problems, who just went berserk—without any kind of forewarning. On the evening news, his neighbors and friends shake their heads in shocked disbelief, because he seemed to be such a fine fellow—Boy Scout leader, caring family man, religious, etc. Somehow he just "snapped." Unfortunately, the story is generally off the front page when everyone's memory begins to improve, such that we find that the subject was not quite as angelic as initially remembered.

Those who specialize in the area of workplace violence or in the threat assessment area in general, generally do not find that people just "snap." There appears to be both a fascination within the culture with the transformation myth (the devil/werewolf/Dracula within us), along with a need to somehow reassure ourselves that there was "nothing that we could have done." It leaves us blameless if we did not anticipate it. How could we? Who could know? This is a critical issue, because it underlies and affects our confidence in any kind of prevention program. Can we prevent something that is subject to an unanticipated "snap"?

Once we begin to analyze these events and review available historic data, information almost invariably begins to emerge, suggesting a pre-existing pattern. Sometimes, a sequence of events is revealed that, when reviewed at any level, represents an ongoing (and often escalating) problem that only now in retrospect becomes obvious to all who are participating in this investigative process.

Along this historical sequence, we often find one or more critical *decision points,* in which awareness and knowledge of the situation were available. At these points, intervention could have occurred that would have diverted the course of events in a relatively less complicated and more benign manner, compared to where we now find ourselves. By not intervening at these critical points, the risks often escalate and become increasingly more difficult to resolve with fewer available options. Certainly the company becomes more liable, as any good attorney can point to these prior events and claim that the company was somehow negligent by not responding appropriately when given the opportunity and the awareness of the problem.

At some point during the investigative process, there is eventually a mutual realization that this situation did not just suddenly erupt from nothing. At some uncomfortable point in the discussion, someone (usually the boss) addresses, in a rather exasperated tone, the question that no one in the room wants to ask (or answer): *"How the heck did we ever let this thing get this far?"*

At that moment or usually before that moment, there is often a general level of embarrassment, when everyone realizes that not only have they allowed the situation to continue for far too long, but that this very avoidance may have served to escalate the problem and increase their risks. Further, by not acting earlier, they no longer have some of the options that may have been available earlier.

In virtually every situation in which we have been involved, multiple bits of information emerged within the presented data, which were previously ignored or were simply wished away. Certainly, we have the benefit of hindsight, but hindsight is only of benefit when and if we do not know what to look for the first time. In many of these cases, the evidence was there and was clear enough if attention had been directed to it. The failure was one of a lack of attention and/or a failure to act.

The Issue of Denial and Avoidance

The primary culprit here is our number one defense mechanism: denial and/or avoidance. When faced with the specter of potentially negative consequences that either we do not want to confront or that simply overwhelm us, we human beings have the ability to protect ourselves from this discomfort by simply ignoring even the obvious, through various defense mechanisms.

These mechanisms are normal and are utilized by all of us on a daily basis. We use them simply because they work as they are intended to work! They protect us from these uncomfortable and unwanted thoughts. Then, if nothing bad happens, we can completely forget our concerns as perhaps unfounded. These are useful defense mechanisms (as they all are) because they help get us through our daily lives with an extra layer of "Teflon." This avoidance becomes a problem when it serves only to postpone (or even escalate) a real risk, by preventing us from preparing ourselves adequately.

You will find throughout the text of this book that an essential element in the prevention of workplace violence is overcoming the natural tendency toward denial and avoidance. Prevention and the successful response to perceived threats of violence are always contingent upon the attention to and recognition of the dangers that exist and the subsequent intentional and planned response.

Violence as a Process

So, despite our denial, do people ever just snap? There are certainly events when an individual's anger may erupt in an explosive, violent response that appears within the immediate context to occur beyond reason. However, as we will discuss in subsequent chapters, *violence does not occur in a vacuum.*

In most of the cases involving workplace violence, we have to examine three broad contributing factors, which will be further detailed in the next chapter:

1) *The individual* (personality and other predisposing characteristics).
2) *The stressors* (and any other triggering mechanisms that are currently increasing the emotional pressure to act).
3) *The setting* within which this all occurs (the situational factors which may serve to either exacerbate or mitigate a violent response).

All three of these elements existed before the individual "snapped." Each of these factors (the individual, the stressors, and the setting) has a history, with observable data. As we will discuss in more detail, violence is not simply an event; it is a result of a developing *process.* Violence is always the result of the interplay among these three elements, and is a part of a broader system, which has to be understood in its entirety. Like a hurricane, it is a spiraling process that is the result of a collision of systems and conditions, all converging at that particular moment. When viewed in this manner, only then can we learn to identify the early events in this development, before it becomes a "critical incident."

Overcoming avoidance and learning to *attend* to potential warning signs is the first and most essential ingredient of any successful prevention and response program. The second ingredient is to once again *overcome avoidance*, after these events have come to our attention, in order to make a decision *to act* on that data. The best action, as will be discussed, may be to decide *not* to take any action, which is a reasonable decision in many circumstances, as long as that indeed represents a *considered decision* and not just a lack of sufficient attention.

> *Our most critical mistakes typically occur not because we made the wrong decision, but because we failed to engage in a decision-making process at all.*

Sometimes this decision-making represents a complex process, and this book may not help the reader who is searching for easy answers. Workplace violence is not a result of an easily identifiable problem that can then be subjected to a cookbook or checklist review for solution. The assessment and management of this problem is one that requires our full attention and resources, along with a willingness to be proactively involved in understanding violence as part of a developing process, and not simply as an event that needs to be doused like an errant flame.

Endnotes

[1] *Daily Labor Report* [BNA], No. 141:A-9 (1994), as reported in Ford & Harrison.
[2] Kaufer & Mattman, "Workplace Violence: An Employer's Guide," as reported in www.noworkviolence.com.
[3] Ibid.
[4] As cited in S. Kaufer, "Corporate Liability: Sharing the Blame for Workplace Violence," as reported in www.noworkviolence.com.
[5] Ibid.

Chapter 2

Who Commits Workplace Violence:
Identifying the At-Risk Employee

"The Profile"

One of the more anticipated segments of our workshops in workplace violence prevention occurs when it comes time to discuss the "characteristics" of the violent or aggressive employee. There is usually a great deal of anticipation that the trainers are prepared to present a "profile," a term that is now widely recognized and utilized by the media.

There is a prevalent belief among the public that somehow those in the general area of forensic/clinical psychology have the ability to accurately predict aggressive behavior based solely on a psychological "profile," generally referring to the personality and demographic characteristics of the individual. Further, there is a belief, or perhaps a wish, that we can now provide a detailed description of a certain personality type that everyone can be on the lookout for, as in a "wanted poster" that we can post on the company's break room bulletin board.

There has been much progress in the research, and there have been some dramatic examples of how forensic behavior specialists have been able to identify and classify characteristics of individuals who have committed certain types of crimes or have engaged in particular forms of violent (usually predatory) behavior. Certainly, many specialists in the general area of threat assessment are indeed well skilled in identifying personality characteristics that may predispose someone to become aggressive in certain situations. Many professionals often have to determine risks based on sometimes very limited data, such as when examining anonymous communications or when presented with objective data about particular individuals of concern.

Our knowledge is not, however, generally sufficient to encompass the various manifestations of violent behavior that occur in the workplace, within a single (or even a few) "profiles," as I hope will become more evident throughout this volume. As already noted in the last chapter, there exist a range of variables that have to be considered when assessing these kinds of risks that go beyond just a consideration of a personality or demographic profile.

We are hard-pressed to give a "workplace violence profile" for essentially three reasons:

1) The relative lack of data. This is not something that has yet undergone a great deal of research, and the data is rather limited.
2) Aggressive behavior is not a single inherent characteristic or trait that we either have or do not have.
3) We are *all* prone to violence *given certain stressors and within certain circumstances* (something that most of us would just as soon prefer not to acknowledge).

As part of our workshop presentation on workplace violence, I often inquire as to how many of the attendees would consider attacking a stranger who attempted to forcefully harm or take their children. After virtually everyone in the audience raises their hand, I then ask how many of them would actually *kill* that other person if that becomes the only way to save their child's life. Rarely does a hand fall. When I ask the attendees how quickly they could become violent in that situation, the response is always that they would most likely respond in a violent manner *instantaneously*—before they could formulate a plan or even a thought, and certainly before they would consider any restraints that their value system may place on them. Are these otherwise psychologically healthy workshop attendees a potentially violent group? Yes indeed!

A far-fetched example? Perhaps, but it certainly demonstrates that we *all* can become lethally violent in a matter of a split second, *if certain conditions were met*. What are the conditions? The conditions in the above-mentioned example of child snatching are very simply that the individual perceived *a threat* to himself or herself or (in this case) a loved one, and also believed that he or she had *no other option*. (Two factors that may be important to keep in mind when defusing or managing many situations, but we are getting ahead of ourselves...)

There are two qualifications that must be understood before discussing the profile of the typical perpetrator of workplace violence:

First of all, workplace violence is not a simple, unitary phenomenon. As has been noted in the previous chapter, violence in the workplace occurs in many forms, serving various motives, and with varying consequences. There are essentially many reasons that individuals respond violently within their employment settings.

Secondly, violence is not simply a result of a personality or demographic "profile." The process of threat or risk assessment is a comprehensive one that has to consider a wide range of data; it is not *just* about identifying personality patterns. Recall our previous reference in the last chapter to the interaction of the three factors of personality, emotional stress, and setting, as *all* being critical when understanding the *process* of violence. As in all human behavior, violence is not a single event that occurs within a vacuum!

So, Do We Have a Profile or Not?

Statistically, if we were to collapse what we know about workplace violence in the United States and feed it into a computer, we would indeed have an average "profile." This profile is largely demographic, relatively general, and not particularly helpful. We know, for example, that most workplace violence has historically been perpetrated mostly by white males in their 40s to 50s who are often described as "loners" and who enjoy firearms. You have no doubt heard this on several occasions from the array of experts interviewed on the news networks during high-profile manhunts.

As a plant manager once noted in one of our workshops, this "profile" described about 70% of his workforce—hardly very useful! Obviously, a profile in this instance is nothing more than a description of common characteristics that a significant number of these individuals have historically shared (for whatever reason) and is hardly specific enough to be of much help. Further, it factors out the many other variables that are not common among past perpetrators, but which may be critical in particular settings.

Even if this describes a large majority of those who have committed workplace violence in the past, it would be foolhardy to overly focus on this particular group and ignore those who would fall outside of it. I know of no investigator who is going to eliminate a 30-year-old Asian woman from consideration, for example, just because she does not fit this description.

By focusing on such a profile, we risk missing important data. The consequences of workplace violence are too great to ignore evidence that is somehow outside the majority of events. Besides, this is historical evidence, and as our society changes, then the results of our research will also undergo some changes. We are, for example, increasingly hearing more concerns about violence by females in the workplace.

Finally, the data that supports the above-mentioned profile represents an extremely small sample of behaviors. Further, it tends to be largely based on workplace homicides, which represent less than *4%* of incidents of *reported* violence, and probably a far smaller percentage of the behaviors that are the focus of this book.

Predicting Violence
The Dynamics of Risk Assessment

From the earliest days of forensic psychology, practitioners have often been asked to "predict" the occurrence of violent behavior. The research has, quite frankly, failed to demonstrate that we are very accurate at that task. Practitioners in this area have generally come to refer to what they do as "threat assessment" or "risk assessment"—two terms that will be used here interchangeably.

This assessment process is not simply an evaluation of the individual's "personality," although that may certainly represent a critical part of this procedure. It is rather a process that examines *all* of the factors that may be contributing to an individual's potential to act in an aggressive or violent manner in that particular situation and at that particular period in time.

Many of the examined factors are *dynamic;* that is, they can (and will often) change over time. Risk assessment itself therefore cannot be static. It takes into account both relatively static and dynamic factors, and always addresses a particular point in time. A good risk assessment should note this temporal aspect—that the conclusions are based on the present set of circumstances. Further, the assessment should ideally address the potential ramifications when and if certain identified dynamic factors were to change.

In regards to violence prediction, recall the simple example above. Almost anyone whose child is attacked is likely to become violent. Violence prediction is therefore ridiculously simple if we do not take into consideration all of the situational and emotional variables that are weighing in at that particular moment, since we are *all* quite capable of engaging in violent behaviors. We differ in our capacity for becoming aggressive, given a certain set of circumstances.

Threat Assessment as a Specialized Process

As noted above, we cannot simply look for standardized profiles, and those who specialize in this area rarely have the benefit of "cookbooks" or prepared templates. The process generally involves the consideration of a wide range of data. This chapter will present an overview of that process. The purpose of this volume is, however, not to teach the reader how to conduct violence risk and threat assessments. This is a complicated and evolving area of specialty that would require more than this chapter. For the threat assessment professional interested in more detailed information, I refer you to excellent works by Corcoran & Cawood (2003), Turner & Gelles (2003), and Reid Meloy (2000), all noted in the bibliography.

This kind of assessment is indeed a specialty area that encompasses an understanding of a broad range of operating variables. This is not an area in which most mental health professionals have had experience, nor is it typically taught in graduate programs. One of the fundamental mistakes committed by organizations, attorneys, and others occurs when a threat assessment is requested from a psychologist or psychiatrist who has little or no experience at this, assuming that all mental health practitioners are equally skilled in this area.

Many mental health professionals also may not have much experience with some of the more common personality disorders that are often encountered in this area. This is particularly problematic when compliance and/or deception are at issue. This again underscores the fact that risk assessment is not simply a psychological evaluation of the individual, and that critical data is generally not solely obtained from an interview or testing process.

The Process of Threat Assessment
An Overview

With the above qualifications, the purpose here is to present a brief review of the relevant factors that are considered in the threat assessment process. If we do not have a "profile" that we can rely on, what information do we review, in order to determine the level of risk that a designated individual is capable of acting violently?

My approach to risk assessment is to determine where an individual is located on a continuum of sorts, in the process of engaging in an aggressive act. More specifically, what are the particular factors (both static and dynamic) that are driving that person toward an act of violence, and what are the factors that may be serving to mitigate or retard that process?

Once this is better understood, then we can better identify the most effective risk management response. The process of risk assessment is nearly always driven by the ultimate question of how to reduce and/or manage the particular threat, in order to ensure safety. Threat assessment and threat management are therefore rarely distinct, linear processes; they often both occur simultaneously and influence each other continually. The assessor instantly becomes part of the *situation* and therefore has an opportunity to influence the level of risk. Conversely, this interaction can operate to change the assessment.

In discussing these risk factors, this is not to imply that this is simply a matter of listing a series of discrete variables, nor is it a matter of adding or subtracting factors to obtain some kind of score. It is important to understand the "whole" of the situation. That includes understanding the "whole" person within the context of this event—what this situation means to that individual and how it relates to his or her history and the broader context of his or her life. We have to understand what has occurred prior to this event, and how these events may be impacting the individual's perception of the future. Further, it is important to comprehend the importance of each of these factors to the subject and the situation in general. Each of these factors is weighted differently, and part of the risk assessment process is to identify the weight or contribution that each of these variables contributes toward the referral question.

In many high-risk incidents, information is obtained from a variety of sources, sometimes directly, but more often through more indirect methods. For our purposes, this information is organized and classified within three generally broad areas, which have previously been identified as "the individual," "the stressors," and "the situation." All of the reviewed information is considered both as discrete factors but also within the context of that individual's life and the context within which this all occurs. As with any attempt to factorize human behavior, the reader will find some overlap, as some of the issues that concern us will show up in more than one of these areas.

The Individual
Static Factors

In this category, our interest is in the individual and what he or she has brought forth to the situation. The focus is on those aspects of the individual that are relatively unchanging—that do not generally vary due to the situational context. Within this category are three primary influences: biological, cultural, and personality.

Biological influences

This is obviously a relatively static area (in terms of our time range of concern) and one over which the individual usually has little control. We do have statistics regarding certain factors, as noted in our discussion of the profile. Being male and in the late teens to early twenties for example, is statistically a higher risk factor for most violence, although, as we have previously noted, most of the extreme violence that has occurred in the workplace up to the present has involved older perpetrators.

An estimate of overall intelligence may be important in that context when determining risk, understanding the subject's experience, planning a response, and interacting with the individual. Also, knowledge of any neurological-based factors such as learning disabilities, attention deficit disorder, etc., may also be of value, especially when the practitioner is involved in an interactive process with the individual. Knowing an individual's educational and/or medical history can help provide this information, but there are often situations in which undiagnosed or relatively mild neurological conditions can significantly impact the individual's behavior. There have been numerous circumstances when it appeared that a learning disability, for example, was responsible for an employee's difficulty with the job requirements, relationships with coworkers, and/or ability to respond appropriately in social interactions.

In this category, we are interested in any biological factor that would impact on the individual's actions, which would include many conditions related to injury or disease, including (but not limited to) mental disorders. The individual may exhibit symptoms of a thought disorder (such as schizophrenia), a biological-based emotional disorder (such as a bipolar disorder), or a neurological disorder involving a degree of brain damage.

Knowing, for example, that an individual has sustained an injury to the frontal lobe of his brain should certainly alert us to the possibility of poor impulse control. In a recent case, it was discovered inadvertently that an individual had a history of multiple seizures that were, at one point, poorly controlled. With this revelation, we began to suspect that some of his actions and his communications were influenced by associated brain damage, which was indeed later confirmed. This understanding substantially influenced the assessment and management of this case, not to mention the legal implications. It certainly changed how others within that organization interpreted and reacted to some of his actions.

The use and abuse of medications, along with illegal substances, could be included here. While this is included elsewhere as a dynamic, more situational influence, drug and alcohol abuse certainly have a biological influence. They may also mimic other conditions. Further, substance use may impact our ability to think, reason, control impulses, etc. Sometimes, substance use may actually be masking other conditions, or may even represent an attempt to compensate or self-treat other mental or physical conditions. Along these lines, it is equally important to investigate the effects of any prescribed medication that may be associated with either mental or physical conditions.

There are many physical and mental conditions that can and will impact the assessment and management process. It is always helpful to review an individual's medical history if at all possible, although even that may not be sufficient. As noted, it pays to be alert to any symptoms that are suggestive of an untreated medical condition. The existence of an untreated condition will certainly often influence our approach, which may then include medical evaluation and treatment. When managing the risks in any of these situations, the management of the medical situation, including substance abuse, often assumes a high priority.

As a final note, a rewarding and unanticipated result of this assessment process occurs when an existing, previously undiagnosed medical condition is identified, for which the subject is subsequently able to obtain treatment. The individual experiences significant and often far-reaching benefits in many aspects of his or her life, including the relationship with the employer.

Cultural/family history

In this area, we are concerned about the environment or culture within which and to which this individual was (and may still be) exposed.

We are interested in individuals' family of origin —the conditions in which they were raised, and their relationships to their parents and siblings. We want to understand their relationship history and the role of aggression in their culture. To what degree was violence relied upon in their family and in the broader community?

We are interested in any other variables that may be important in understanding the subject's predisposition to use violence as a means of expression or control, particularly in situations that have similarities to the one in question. It is equally beneficial to understand his or her peer group, from childhood to the present. Certainly, involvement in certain political or religious groups may increase risks in some situations. Part of the cultural understanding also includes an understanding of the person's history and interest in the use of weapons, and how much that may or may not be related to his or her cultural background.

As will be discussed under the section on personality, one of the best predictors of future violence is past violence. Understanding not only the person's individual history, but also how aggression was perceived and practiced within the culture that has nurtured him or her, is a critical part of the process.

Personality

For the purposes of this discussion, "personality" is defined as those rather enduring traits and characteristics that help us to define the individual. We are particularly interested in the usual and characteristic manner in which the person relates to the world about him. Within the social context, it specifically refers to how he perceives and relates to others.

This does not refer to an individual's emotional "state," which is more variable, but which is certainly influenced by aspects of his or her personality. The focus here is on a relatively static or stable phenomenon. As much as we may attempt to control it or compensate for it, our personality generally changes relatively little in our adult years.

It is clear from this definition that we are speaking of something that has manifested itself historically. Even with all of our psychological assessment devices and personality inventories, the best predictor of future behavior remains quite simply, *past behavior*. This is particularly true when assessing the risk of violence. There always exist patterns of behavior that are, to some degree, discoverable.

The most useful information comes with an understanding of individuals' social relationships: how they develop, maintain, and exit relationships. Do they have a support system? How do they relate to others in the workplace? How do they react to conflict, disagreement, or the ambiguity of relationships? People's social behavior will be reflected in their behavior with their coworkers, their supervisors, and their employer in general.

Risk assessment is not a matter of establishing the existence of some kind of personality disorder, nor is the intent of this kind of assessment to diagnose mental disorders. However, it is safe to say that many incidents of workplace violence are committed by individuals who exhibit traits that would reach the level that psychologists and psychiatrists define as "personality" or "character" disorders. Personality traits become "disorders" when they become severely maladaptive, inflexible and/or distressful for the individual.

There are many personality traits and/or disorders that are of particular interest to those who conduct threat assessments. The existence of a history that suggests antisocial, paranoid, or various social attachment disorders, for example, will generally impact our assessment and guide the management process significantly. Conversely, some personality patterns may serve to mitigate the risk of violence, such as those that suggest a history of passivity or avoidance of conflict, for example.

Once again, the risk assessment process is not a diagnostic one. Any interest in an individual's character is governed by the safety concerns of that particular situation. We are less interested in diagnostic categories than we are in determining how the subject is likely to react to certain stressors, situations, and other stimuli that may be represented in the situation of concern. Needless to say, this understanding will, in turn, significantly influence response planning decisions.

The "Overly Attached" Employee

I never will forget the interview that I had with an individual whose employment had been terminated one year earlier. He was hurt and furious with his former employer, and had subsequently engaged in a campaign of threats and retaliatory acts. Toward the end of the interview, I asked him if he knew what the time was, at which point he proudly displayed a wristwatch that was prominently engraved with the company's logo. When we parted and I asked for his telephone number, he handed me his old business card, kept in a clip, which was also engraved with the company's logo.

After a year of unemployment, he remained angry with his former employer, but he also so identified with the company that he was virtually unable to even consider looking for another job, despite offers of outplacement counseling and other resources. Working for this company *defined* him and provided his only sense of purpose. After all those years on the road for this employer, his social life essentially existed only through his work. As he had literally no sense of identity separate from this employer, he could not effectively detach and face the void that awaited him.

Dr. Harley Stock has identified what he terms *"pathological organizational affective attachment"* to describe those individuals who are so bonded to their workplace that they essentially cannot "let go," sometimes even *years* after the termination of their employment.[1] This individual is so attached to the organization, that he or she literally cannot separate in a complete and reasonable manner, and may subsequently respond with anger and threats, fueled by feelings of abandonment and betrayal, far beyond what is typically experienced by the average terminated employee. This is a prolonged and extreme type of dependency that represents underlying social attachment problems that are likely manifested in other areas of the individual's life, and actually represents a significant portion of employee-related threats of violence.

The Effect of Stress
Emotional Aspects

Most of the individuals identified in workplace violence incidents are under a significant degree of stress. While we may have concerns about underlying, ongoing personality factors, there is typically a strong emotional component. There is often a grievance, a traumatizing event, or an ongoing situation that is distressing the subject and increasing the risk of an aggressive reaction *at that particular moment in time*, especially in those who are predisposed to react aggressively by nature of their personality structure.

Understanding the degree and nature of their distress within the context of their personality and the situational components is always critical, if only because it is critical to the individual. Understanding the related stressors and how they impact the individual is an integral part of both the assessment and the management process.

While the threat of "affective violence" (as opposed to the more calculated predatory violence) is easier to manage ultimately, that is not to say it represents less of a danger. The right approach can critically and quickly defuse and resolve the issue, while the wrong response can send it all into an uncontrollable spiral.

Many of these individuals have experienced significant loss. They have often displayed signs of depression and other signs of emotional distress. They have almost always left numerous clues along the way. They may be asking for help, or have had repeated requests for help ignored. They are often angry and believe that they have been treated unfairly, or that they have been betrayed or abused in some manner. Many are, very simply, seeking justice.

The stress may come from the workplace or outside the workplace, but it is significant that the triggering event has almost always been historically something that occurs *in the workplace!*

Many of these threats have been part of a "cry for help," just as there has been a suicidal component in many fatal workplace incidents. This may be much like the "suicide by cop" scenario that law enforcement encounters when subjects engage in an action with the ultimate goal being to have themselves killed in the process. Unfortunately, they often do not mind taking others with them.

Sometimes a relatively small amount of intervention can be helpful, if addressed early enough. Certainly, the effect of emotional stress underscores the importance of identifying these individuals or addressing the source of their stress as early as possible. The benefit of Employee Assistance Programs (EAPs) and such cannot be overemphasized.

This is not to imply that most of these incidents involve individuals undergoing the normal adjustment process to a stressful event. Generally, these incidents come to our attention because they involve individuals with a maladaptive history—individuals who may be more predisposed, by nature of their personality structure, to react aggressively to that which they experience as distressing. Their behavior and their internal construction of events may have created or exacerbated the stressful situation, or may be influencing their interpretation of events.

That which the individual *perceives* as stressful, and how that individual *reacts* to stress, is the critical concern. Regardless of the source of the stress, stress reduction is generally a primary part of any risk management plan. Understanding the above-mentioned personality dynamics of that individual will be critical, because stress is always an experience that is dependent on one's interpretation of events.

"The Disgruntled Employee"

While not part of any standardized typology, the "disgruntled employee" is a phrase that has emerged within the media and has now become quite widely utilized among the public. This is for good reason, as it does represent the subjective perception of a significant portion of employee-initiated violence, and—in its extreme form—fits the description of some of better-known incidents that have been reported in the media.

Dr. Todd Conklin of the Los Alamos National Laboratory defines the *"disgruntled"* employee as an individual who believes that he or she has been unfairly treated (typically based on a core past trauma), who is obsessively focused on this grievance or trauma, and who has come to the conclusion that there exists no mechanisms within the company to address these core issues.[2] This employee has become increasingly

---

alienated and egocentric, and has essentially decided to take things into his or her own hands.

Dr. Conklin has further identified a progression of three stages that certain employees will traverse, if the company does not take appropriate action, before eventually arriving at the point of "disgruntled," where they represent a significant safety risk.

The first stage is the *"disillusioned"* stage, which describes most of us at various points in our relationship with our employers. The disillusioned employee is not happy with his or her employer, and may indeed be deeply disappointed about career advancement or any work-related issue. This person may question whether he or she should be employed and may even have doubts about whether the dissatisfaction can be resolved. Most do resolve these issues internally and are able to return to what is their emotional baseline. They may or may not have had their concerns addressed to their satisfaction, but they have found a way to cope with the situation adequately enough, such that they can remain effectively employed.

Those who cannot resolve this and cannot return to a feeling of relative emotional stability may become obsessed with what they perceive as blatantly unfair treatment. There is usually an original trauma or grievance or conflict that they cannot forget or forgive. They become more and more obsessed and more alienated from the company, such that they become *"disaffected."* They begin to see themselves as alone against a larger entity, and with relatively few options. Their moods and general relationships with their coworkers deteriorate as they isolate themselves further. Their goals and their motivations become more egocentric and begin to deviate from the organization.

The *"disgruntled"* employee, as noted above, represents the final stage, when the employee has essentially lost all hope that there exist options within the organization to resolve his or her grievance. This person has come to believe that the organization, or individuals within the organization, are solely responsible for all of his or her unhappiness. Feeling somehow emotionally "cornered," the individual feels compelled to take aggressive and/or retaliatory action.

Most employees are familiar with their "disgruntled" coworkers, and generally recognize the "disaffected" as well. However, these problem employees engender such a high level of concern that most of their coworkers (and supervisors) react to them in the only way they know how to safely do so: by avoiding them. No one wants to do or say anything to upset them any further. As such, they become more and more alienated and ostracized. Eventually, they become a feared unknown, a quiet time bomb. The initial newspaper reports will imply that he "exploded" unexpectedly, but subsequent interviews will confirm that his coworkers all knew that "something eventually would happen."

Situational Factors

Situational factors refer to those events external to the individual that are occurring in his or her environment. These may be events that are internal or may be external to the organization, such as with domestic and community issues. The threat assessment process cannot ignore the setting or context within which the behavior is occurring. Likewise, understanding those factors within and outside the organization may provide knowledge and assistance in the management and resolution process.

It is often difficult to initially know what may or may not be important for our purposes; so the goal of the investigation process should be to know *as much as possible* about the subject's personal life and background. Understanding the subject's support system and what is occurring within that support system is often most critical, especially when management options are being considered. Having knowledge of the existence and effect of recent traumas, anticipated losses, financial crises, etc. can all contribute to the threat assessment process. Understanding the person's activities, hobbies, relationships, and outside sources of stress are all part of this process. It is difficult to enumerate a list of potentially important information, because any bit of information could be of use in the threat assessment and management process.

It goes without saying that understanding the internal, organizational context within which this behavior occurs is critical. Workplace violence, as noted above, is almost always triggered by an event that occurs in the workplace. This event may be part of a longstanding issue, grievance, or conflict. We have been involved in multiple incidents of threat that were in response to a poorly-considered remark or action by a supervisor. It should always be noted that if an individual feels abused or mistreated in the workplace, we cannot automatically assume that this is all the result of the subject's misperception. The targeted individual or victim's role is often a critical part of the investigation.

Understanding any loss that the individual may be experiencing will be important information. Certainly, if the company is to terminate an employee of concern, then understanding that loss within the context of their residual resources is critical knowledge. If the company encounters retaliatory behaviors after terminating an employee without severance or assistance, and if their subsequent investigation reveals a 30-year employee with a history of working overtime in order to avoid losing his home due to expenses incurred from his deceased wife's medical bills, it should not require a psychologist to explain the reasons for this individual's emotional response to this event (although unfortunately, sometimes it does!)

When examining important external issues, it is imperative that the investigator considers anything that could impact the *means* of committing violence. Certainly, this includes the person's ownership, knowledge, and experience with weapons. Any behavior suggesting addiction, substance abuse, or engagement in other self-destructive activities such as gambling may be important.

Critical Elements in Threat Communications

There are critical elements embedded in the communication of the threat and within the historical data that will provide the threat assessment specialist with a better understanding of how far along the subject is on this hypothetical continuum toward a violent response. Individuals engage in violence for different reasons, but at some level, it occurs because the subject has come to perceive violence as a viable solution that will, in some way, address a perceived problem or need.

As will be discussed further in Chapter 5, threats and threatening behavior themselves serve some kind of purpose. They may simply be an expressive discharge of emotion, or a way to regulate internal stress (to prevent a violent response), or the threat may be an act to accomplish some sort of effect. While there are individuals who use threats routinely as a means of controlling others, threats and/or the violent act itself often serve to help the subject regain a sense of control. And there are those who use threats or engage in threatening behavior as a kind of advance warning. In short, the threat assessment professional must understand the nature and intent of the threat, within both the broader and the more immediate context of the subjects' lives, along the dimensions as described above.

There are elements of the threat that will suggest how close this individual may be to committing an act of violence, and who therefore may be at greater risk. The subject's *focus* on particular, identified targets—as opposed to a more amorphous, generalized sense of resentment—will suggest a higher risk, and that the subject may be closer to engagement. Likewise, a subject who has arrived at a relatively narrow *fixation* that is organized around a belief that attributes most, if not all, of his or her problems to this target represents a higher degree of risk.

Any threat or history that includes a greater degree of *specificity, detailed planning,* or *rehearsal* is certainly of greater concern, as is any communication that suggests a pressure, or *an imperative* to act, or to act within a particular time frame. It is important to have knowledge of the subject's overall engagement in any attack-related behaviors. This may include, but is not limited to, increased use of violence, engagement in "approach behaviors," obsession with weaponry, or commitment to take action to what is believed to be an otherwise irresolvable problem.

In understanding the purpose of the threatening behavior, the subject's view of his or her future is critical. Someone with a recent history of significant losses may believe that he or she literally has nothing else to lose. The subject may feel so threatened by circumstances within and outside that context, that he or she is literally in a survival mode, fighting for self-preservation. An act of violence may represent a desperate attempt to regain control in a life with no other perceived options. The act may also represent some part of a greater mission or divine plan, whether it is a particular religious belief or simply "justice," suggesting that the subject is less concerned about his or her own well-being, and willing to sacrifice to a greater cause.

All of this is to again emphasize that while our research is progressing and is continually identifying the more critical variables that should be considered in threat assessment, any threat or threatening behavior has to be *understood* within both the historical and immediate context of that particular individual in that particular situation at that specific point in time.

Warning Signs

This chapter began with a discussion that discouraged reliance on restrictive and over-simplified profiles. Nevertheless, we will conclude the chapter with a list of the more common signs that have been historically encountered in incidents of workplace violence, but not without some comments and qualifications.

The reader has probably seen most of these listed in various other texts. Some may be signs that would be of obvious concern, while others may be general and relatively common to some degree. This list generally is composed either of signs and symptoms of individuals undergoing significant distress or of individual characteristics that may predispose that individual to a violent response.

These have been organized into 13 of what I believe to represent the most serious and the most common antecedent behaviors, based on the experience of myself and other practitioners in this area. None of these behaviors in and of themselves should denote that an individual would become violent, although all of these should produce a level of concern that warrants our attention. Nonviolent people can certainly exhibit some of these behaviors. Nor is this an exclusive list. Just because someone does not exhibit these behaviors does not suggest that he or she will not become aggressive.

Many of these behaviors should be more strongly considered if they represent a significant change in the individual's usual habits and/or demeanor. For example, the use and interest in weaponry is often most critical if it represents a sudden increase in use and interest for this particular individual, in light of other behaviors.

Common Antecedents of Workplace Violence

1. *History of aggressive behavior.* This includes any and all acts of aggression historically, and as exhibited in the workplace. Individuals who have a history of attempting to control others by intimidation by threats and threatening behavior are of particular concern.
2. *Social isolation and poor peer relationships.* Because we are social beings, the lack of a stable social support system is always of concern and implies that the individual is without a significant stabilizing influence. Hence the often accurate stereotype of the "loner" in workplace violence incidents.
3. *Decreased and inconsistent productivity.* This includes not only decreased productivity, but also related behaviors such as increased absences, tardiness, loss of motivation,

impaired concentration, etc.—all indicative of severe emotional distress and/or decompensation.

4. ***Signs of emotional distress.*** The list of behaviors would be too numerous to include here, and is generally self-evident to most of us, if we are paying attention. Increased irritability, moodiness, and social withdrawal are examples of signs that suggest increased emotional distress.

5. ***Abnormal obsessions.*** This includes any obsessive ideation that may represent a breakdown in the individual's psychological functioning. He or she may be obsessed with an individual, an event, or a highly specific religious or world view. This implies a phenomenon that has recently emerged or has increased in intensity, to a degree that it affects the individual's socialization and adaptive skills. Certainly, the content of the obsessions and whether the obsessions compel a response may influence the degree of potential risk.

6. ***Unstable work history.*** Someone who has a history of job changes that are otherwise unexplainable may suggest a pattern of work-related relationship problems that may not have been otherwise apparent.

7. ***Fascination with weapons or with violent events.*** "Fascination" with weapons should not be confused with "interest in" or "ownership of" weapons. As with other signs listed here, we are most concerned with whether there has been a recent and significant increase in the degree of interest. Also, any fascination or obsession with violence in general or with episodes of violence, especially those that have occurred in workplace settings, has been a historically significant antecedent.

8. ***Substance abuse.*** Increased substance use not only indicates the existence of underlying emotional problems, but also may also facilitate an aggressive action and increase risks substantially. Many believe that substance abuse is a very common underlying factor in workplace violence incidents, more than is often recognized or identified.

9. *Paranoia.* While this is a clinical term, signs that are commonly identified as "paranoia" are often of concern and raise the possibility that the individual may misinterpret the behaviors in others, leading to possible defensive reactions. These behaviors may include hypervigilence, extreme social sensitivity, feelings of persecution, ideas of reference (i.e. people are talking about him), attributing blame inappropriately, etc.

10. *Coworkers are afraid.* The employee's peers are the ones who know the subject employee the best. Many times, other employees have a "gut feeling" and find themselves avoiding that individual whenever possible. They may dread coming to work because of that individual. In many past instances of workplace violence, this kind of fear existed among the coworkers prior to the event. This may represent an internal alarm system that may be reacting to other signs at a subconscious level.

11. *Changes in personality.* This is another sign that suggests that a very significant psychological decompensation process is occurring. A normally meticulous dresser starts to come in to work in dirty fatigues; a jovial employee becomes withdrawn and quiet; a polite, passive individual becomes suddenly abusive and irritable—all of these and any other variations are often worth our attention.

12. *Deterioration in self-care.* Sudden changes in how an individual takes care of him- or herself, in terms of hygiene, appearance, eating habits, etc. are typically indicative of severe depression or other severe psychological disturbances. There is typically an accompanying change in the person's social interactions and overall energy level.

13. *Chronic grievances.* This refers to individuals who continually complain, to the point that they have become chronic "victims." They suffer from "attribution bias," a psychological term that simply means that they tend to blame others for their problems, rarely taking much personal responsibility for events that they perceive as happening "to" them.

A Final Word about Warning Signs

Threat assessment in critical situations is ultimately best left up to those who are identified and trained in this area. However, the most critical component in workplace violence prevention is the early identification of the precursors of violence, which can precipitate a threat assessment and response process before anyone is hurt.

Training managers and other employees to recognize "profiles" is of little value in violence prevention. A more effective prevention measure would be to train employees to recognize signs of distress, along with any behaviors that could facilitate an act of aggression.

To effectively prevent workplace violence, managers and other employees should be trained to become more cognizant of any aberrant or unusual behaviors that could potentially suggest a troubled or high-risk employee. We expect many "false positives," that is, we expect that we will be referred individuals who are not ultimately determined to represent a risk of violence. This is always a preferred alternative to the culture of denial that exists in many organizational contexts.

We cannot expect our employees to engage in risk assessment. However, we can expect the organization to establish a process whereby potential problems are identified early. All of the signs mentioned here are observable and generally knowable by the company's employees if they are attentive and have been trained as to how and when to report critical observables. Each individual employee is therefore a critical part of this process.

Endnotes

[1] R. Clay, "Securing the Workplace: Are Our Fears Misplaced?" *Monitor on Psychology*, 31, 9, (2000).

[2] T. Conklin, personal communication, 2000.

Chapter 3

Common Errors and Oversights
(What You Do Not Want to Hear)

If one wishes to understand anything or anyone, it helps to attend to the recurring patterns in communication and behavior. Likewise, to understand how an organization arrives at a point where it finds itself confronting a risk of violence, it may be useful to identify those common patterns of mistakes and omissions that repeatedly occur.

In this chapter, I will be listing the comments and *phrases* that I, and most other professionals in this area, most frequently encounter when reviewing situations involving a workplace threat. I have in the past, found this to be a more effective learning tool than simply providing "to do" and "to not do" lists.

Most of these comments occur frequently enough that they would probably be statistically significant if we were to somehow record and analyze our various interactions when involved in these situations. Most practitioners in this area have heard them enough that we are seldom surprised when they occur, although they can still at times cause us to shake or heads in disbelief or frustration. These phrases are often a reflection of the natural responses and defense mechanisms that we humans will instinctually utilize when faced with adversity.

Most of these statements represent a breakdown in the organization's prevention system, such that potentially dangerous situations have been allowed to continue and even escalate. Any effective prevention system has to be able to override these kinds of common (and perhaps natural) responses. As will be discussed in this and the next chapter, all can be effectively addressed by the organization.

"He just kind of snapped."
Overcoming Denial

As already discussed in a previous chapter, those who regularly respond to threatening or violent behaviors rarely if ever find that people suddenly engage in a violent response without some kind of warning signs along the way. Instead of someone who "snaps," we instead typically uncover a pattern of behaviors that predated this particular event, but which were apparently ignored, denied, or somehow explained away. However, whenever we are asked to respond to a perceived threat, the request is usually presented as a recent event that has just surfaced. There is often a flurry of activity and anxiety to deal with this *new* sense of danger, when a subsequent investigation very quickly uncovers a pre-existing or long-developing danger.

The impact of denial and avoidance on workplace violence will not be belabored here, as this has been discussed and will continue to be alluded to throughout this volume. In fact, many of the phrases presented in this chapter are manifestations of these particular defense mechanisms.

> *In order to be effective, an organization's workplace violence program must include a process that helps its members overcome the natural tendency to ignore or dismiss early warning signs.*

"How did we let this thing get this far?"
The Culture of Avoidance

This statement generally occurs during the course of the initial review. A rather embarrassed realization becomes conscious: that the organization has had access to and knowledge of behaviors that have left them vulnerable, by this point, in a number of different ways. The subject indeed did not "just snap."

This represents a potentially embarrassing moment for almost everyone involved, and there is often plenty of blame to go around. Whereas this statement is typically uttered by those in charge, and whereas management sometimes would like to discover a single root source of negligence on which to place the blame, it is more often than not a result of a widely-practiced system of avoidance that reflects the corporate culture. It is rarely a conscious act or pattern, and it may even be contrary to the company's *stated* policy.

If managers discover that their people ignored critical, reportable events, it suggests a pattern of learned inaction, which has probably occurred at multiple points and at multiple levels. Rarely do we encounter incidents in which there was only one member of the organization who had failed to properly respond. Further, the longer the subject engaged in the questionable behaviors, the more everyone assumed that it was somehow permissible. Ultimately, no one was willing to step forward and blow the whistle on something that appeared allowed or even sanctioned.

The organization must commit to a culture in which each and every employee is expected to respond in a designated, well-defined manner if they encounter inappropriate or potentially high-risk behaviors.

"Why did we hire this guy in the first place?"
Keeping Dangerous People Out

Frequently, investigation of the individual's history reveals a pattern of violent or otherwise high-risk behaviors that had occurred *before he or she was hired*. Sometimes, these were discovered through a background investigation or simply by a few follow-up phone calls, prompted by evidence in the original application form on file. There have been times when it has been as simple as noticing some inconsistencies in an individual's past employment record. Phone calls to past supervisors (that included a direct and persistent line of questioning) uncovered information that could have saved the company a great deal if known *before the subject was hired.*

Certainly, it is difficult in this day to obtain the information that we would like, as former employers are often inclined to provide little information as a matter of policy, often limited to confirmation of employment and dates of employment. While this certainly represents a barrier, many times, the right kind of questioning to the right individuals can at least surface some suggestions of concern that can be subsequently investigated more thoroughly.

If we can take this same information (i.e., the employee's application form, background report, etc.) and ferret out problematic information regarding the applicant's history when investigating a threat, then that process is equally available during the hiring process. Sometimes it may be a matter of investigative expertise, but more often than not, it is a result of some oversights during the hiring process.

Once again, the culprit here is usually the mechanism of denial in the broad sense. When hiring, we often feel a sense of pressure to fill a vacuum that exists in our organization. The selection process is often a long and complicated one, and sometimes occurs long after the vacuum has been created. We want more than anything else to get the position filled, to relieve some of the workload or backlog that has developed. The hiring process itself diverts us even more from our work, so we want to believe that the applicant who is sitting across the desk from us will be perfect for the job.

We may wish that to be true so much that we may rush through the process and see and hear just what we want to see and hear. We may focus on the applicant's positive characteristics and overlook or explain away the negative ones. We may even rush through the reference checks, requesting only a quick affirmation, and be willing to accept limited information, as if "no news is good news." When we have asked references why they did not reveal this information the first time, we often have been informed that they were not given the time to do so, or were not even asked.

There are ways in which the company can be more careful in the hiring process, as will be discussed in the next chapter. Companies should consult with their attorneys as to what they can or cannot address in the hiring process, and should use whatever is at their disposal. As discussed in Chapter 1, organizations may be considered negligent if they hire a dangerous employee without an appropriate review. Further, legal consultation may be important if a potentially violent employee is released. There have been successful lawsuits due to negligent referencing claims, when a former employer failed to alert the hiring company of its concerns about the risk of violence.[1]

A company should take all the precautions legally available to it to ensure that it does not bring a dangerous person into the workplace.

"We don't have anything in the file."
The Value of Documentation

In some of our referred cases, the company has long been aware of and concerned about the actions of a problem employee. From the beginning, we are informed that the company is simply "fed up" with this employee, who may have a long history of intimidating, threatening, or otherwise inappropriate behavior. Sometimes, these employees may have actually been confronted and counseled about this behavior. However, when we ask to review the contents of the employee's file, the response is sometimes a quiet, embarrassed, "Well, there is nothing really in his file." A review of the file confirms that there is indeed *nothing in the file!*

Documentation is important for a number of reasons. If nothing else, it certainly will protect the company if the company takes some kind of employment action, and if there are then subsequent legal questions about the company's motivations.

Focusing on the psychological aspects, we urge and encourage documentation for a different reason. Very simply, documentation helps to *override the natural tendency toward avoidance, denial, and indecision.* If it accomplishes nothing else, documentation will serve to force a degree of awareness that will be difficult to overlook or ignore. Further, repeated documentation in one's file helps to alert us to patterns that may otherwise be considered as discrete events when observed by various managers.

Documentation also facilitates decision-making. It is less likely that a manager will enter a description of inappropriate behavior without also documenting the subsequent action (or inaction). Putting things in writing often ensures accountability. Even if the manager *decides* ("decides" being the key word here) that the behavior does not warrant a response, subsequent repeated documentation will eventually alert someone of a pattern that may require a different response. This, in turn, can serve to prompt discussions with fellow managers, eventually helping to raise awareness and facilitate a coordinated, planned approach.

Documentation can help the company be more accountable. It will result in an earlier and a greater degree of awareness and attention to potential problems, and will subsequently facilitate a more decisive and less avoidant response.

"We can always just call the police."
The One-Stop Solution

Including this statement in my list of problem phrases should in no way imply that one should not contact law enforcement if there is a perceived threat of violence. Alerting and working in cooperation with local law enforcement is an important and often critical part of the company's response plan.

There are a couple of critical issues here. First is that there is no *one* response that can serve as the first or only item on our menu whenever confronted with a threat of violence. This statement is typically uttered by a company that has no Threat Response Plan and has yet to encounter this kind of situation, believing somehow that calling the police represents an easy solution.

We have already discussed how varied the phenomenon of workplace violence can be. Further, a reported threat always exists within a context that must be carefully considered. In all situations involving a threat of violence, it is critical that any action (or inaction) be considered in light of the possible consequences. Calling local law enforcement to alert them of certain activities should be accomplished when it is part of a plan that considers the potential consequences of that decision.

It may be that law enforcement cannot act in the manner that we would prefer. If there has not been a crime committed, and if the purpose of sending law enforcement is to investigate or intimidate the individual, then certainly one needs to be cognizant of the potential consequences of that contact. If law enforcement officials do not understand the situation or if there is not an ongoing cooperative relationship between the company and the local police, then this may result in a situation in which we are working at crossed purposes.

If we are asking the police to confront this individual, what are we actually asking them to do? If the person is not going to be in police custody, what is going to be the result of that confrontation? Most importantly, are there any chances that this referral and subsequent contact may actually increase, as opposed to reduce, the risks?

This is certainly also true of any legal action, such as protective or temporary restraining orders. Whereas a protective order may be quite appropriate in many situations, one has to consider carefully the inflammatory possibilities and the consequences for those named in that order.

> *Law enforcement cannot serve as the company's single response to a threat of workplace violence. However, it is imperative that the organizations establish a cooperative, working relationship with their local law enforcement agency and its individual officers, so that they can better understand your needs and can work cooperatively with the organization when the need arises.*

"We referred him to an EAP."
Another One-Stop Solution

Employee Assistance Programs (EAPs) are always highly recommended and certainly are critical and useful in any kind of workplace violence prevention program. The research confirms that if an employee has an opportunity to address ongoing stress in his or her life, then the chance of that stress negatively impacting the workplace is much reduced.

Employees are always benefited when provided assistance with the situational crises in their lives before they have a chance to escalate. However, there is a tendency at times to believe that an EAP referral represents the sole and comprehensive solution to a problem involving potential workplace violence. In some cases, when we have asked how the company has responded to a particular ongoing situation, their response is that they have referred the employee to an EAP. There is often an implication that the responsibility for resolving this employee's "problem" and rendering him or her harmless has been passed along to the EAP and that the employer's role in the process has been completed.

In these situations, there was rarely adequate follow-up and there was no communication with the EAP provider, as is normally the case, since this typically represents a confidential relationship. There is sometimes a feeling of assurance that the EAP counselor will alert the company if there is a potential for harm. However, this will occur if and only if the employee actually is compliant with the appointments and if and only if that counselor has the expertise, information, and time to make that determination.

There are several pitfalls here:

1. Simply referring the individual anywhere as a routine response is never sufficient. As discussed above, there is seldom a simple, single response that can be utilized when assessing a potentially violent individual.
2. Referring an individual anywhere as part of a planned response without following up in order to ascertain that the employer's concerns were addressed is insufficient and negligent.
3. Due to the legitimate concerns about confidentiality, Employee Assistance Programs are not often in a position to advise and adequately address the company's concerns. Further, they may not be capable of assessing the problem from the company's perspective, as their perspective is generally that of an individual counselor. Mental health professionals are not always experienced in working with a third party, regarding the third party's interests.
4. Mental health providers specialize in different areas, and referral does not guarantee that the provider's expertise is in the area of the company's concern or that the employee is utilizing the EAP in the manner anticipated.
5. The areas of threat assessment and threat management represent very particular specialties that are not common among mental health professionals, nor are they common among organizations that provide short-term, supportive mental health care.

6. Finally, many mental health professionals do not have experience in working with certain personality disorders or with cases that may involve deception. Deception is often not a critical issue in most counseling practices that treat self-referred clients.

The Employee Assistance Program can be a critical and important part of the solution process, but cannot represent the organization's sole response in high-risk situations.

"We did not want to make him angry."
Avoiding Confrontation

In cases involving threats of violence in the workplace, a significant percentage of referred employees could be described as, for a lack of a better term, "bullies." Every workplace has its share of employees who will use intimidation to get their way. This is often part of a strategy of control that is generally effective. The result is that their coworkers avoid them, and their supervisors may even avoid disciplining them. Everyone simply stays out of their way and gives them a wide berth in everything they do. This kind of employee exists in most employment settings where the employer has not verbalized a clear commitment not to tolerate this kind of hostile behavior.

Unfortunately, avoidance does not eliminate the problem behavior. In fact, the behavior is reinforced and is allowed to escalate over time if it is not confronted and appropriately addressed. When interviewed, these employees are occasionally (and legitimately) astounded that others find them intimidating. They have never received any feedback about the effects of their behavior, and they may be sufficiently egocentric so as to not be aware of the reactions and feelings of others.

Sometimes these employees are shifted throughout the organization and transferred from one division to another. The organization and their coworkers have discovered a variety of methods in order to avoid confrontation, for fear of inflaming them. These methods are eventually doomed to failure, as the company is just postponing the inevitable.

Even when a decision is made to terminate the employee, employers oftentimes want to enact a threat assessment process that avoids any possibility that the employee discovers their concerns. Sometimes, they attempt to find other reasons for dismissal to avoid dealing with him directly.

It is important that the company *not avoid its established disciplinary process*. Meetings with these employees should be documented, and they should be informed of the consequences for continued inappropriate behavior. If this is communicated in a direct and clear manner by the company to a recently-hired employee, he or she may decide that this is not the place to stay and may actually find some way to exit the organization peacefully. But for long-term employees, the avoidance of discipline provides them with a sense of entitlement that makes their eventual separation from the company increasingly difficult as time goes by.

It is critical that the organizations confront and discipline abusive and intimidating employees immediately, and overcome any tendencies to postpone or avoid these interactions.

"We just didn't take him seriously."
When Employees Assess Threats

When we discover that the employee has a history of unreported threatening behavior, we often interview coworkers as part of our investigation. When we inquire as to why they avoided reporting their observations, it is sometimes shrugged off as "no big deal."

Certainly, not all threats or threatening behavior represent a serious risk, and this statement may reflect the coworker's honest opinion that this event did not represent a serious threat. However, this employee also may be subject to the same sort of denial previously discussed, and for the same reasons. The above statement also may represent a rationalization, to justify why he or she did not report the behavior. No one prefers to believe that a coworker is dangerous, and no one wants to go to the trouble of actually making that report, with all the possible consequences. It is far easier to shrug it off and rationalize it as a "joke" or a rare outburst.

Regardless and perhaps most importantly for our purposes, the implication of this statement is that this coworker believes that it is his or her duty to first determine whether the threat is of concern and therefore legitimate *before* coming forth to report that concern. This puts an unrealistic burden and places the employee in a role of making threat assessments. Threat assessment is best left up to those so designated. If an employee believes that he or she cannot refer even the smallest concerns to the responsible authority without risking some embarrassment or some kind of judgment regarding the appropriateness of the report, then any prevention program will not be effective.

> *Employees must understand that any and all concerns need to be reported, and that these concerns will be investigated in a careful, confidential, and professional manner.*

"That's just the way he/she is."
So Far, So Good...

This is one of my favorite rationalizations, and one of the more puzzling if placed under the microscope of reason. The company receives reports of some very problematic behaviors exhibited by a particular employee, behaviors that may include abuse, intimidation, or even violence. When interviewed, their coworkers or supervisors will grin and shake their heads, or shrug in a gesture of powerlessness, and say by way of some kind of explanation, "Yeah, that's just the way he is" or "That's just Joe." Everyone then nods in agreement sympathetically, as if somehow that all reassures and justifies our inaction. Some reassurance!

What that statement really implies is that because this behavior has not led to disaster *yet,* it will therefore (hopefully) not occur in the future. This statement also implies that this is somehow out of our control and therefore *cannot* be legitimately addressed, justifying our sense of helplessness. As noted above, bullying or intimidating behavior will be reinforced and can escalate when confrontation is avoided. To some degree, this employee may have participated in or promoted this perception. He has somehow communicated a belief that he cannot adapt or change this behavior, because "that's just the way I am" (i.e. "Take it or leave it!")

We cannot dismiss someone's inappropriate behavior as somehow outside the realm of our control. Further, believing that nothing "real bad" will occur because this is all just part of the subject's personality (as evidenced by the fact that nothing bad has yet occurred) is simply not a reasonable conclusion.

All signs of potentially violent behavior should undergo an assessment process. If inappropriate behavior is ignored, it should be for reasons other than because of "the way he is."

"She just hasn't been herself lately."
When Employees Are Troubled

Whenever we train employees and managers to become more aware of the warning signs of potential violence, one category that we discuss is what we term "aberrant behavior." The dictionary defines "aberrant" as that which "deviates from what is normal or typical."

When an individual is undergoing a great deal of stress that has overwhelmed his or her coping skills, one sometime sees dramatic changes in the person's appearance, behavior, or communication with others. If these changes are significant and sustained, then there may be concerns that this individual is undergoing an adjustment process in which he or she has exhausted all resources.

This *does not* automatically imply that they are potentially violent or represent a risk to other employees, but it could be an indication of something that needs to be reviewed, at first on an informal level. It certainly should not be ignored. Many of the more well-known incidences involving workplace violence have included observations by coworkers that the individual had began coming into work disheveled, dressed inappropriately, or engaging in inappropriate social behavior, sometimes as minor as being irritable or reclusive toward others.

Being aware of the signs of a troubled employee, such as dramatic shifts in an employee's behavior or a sudden decrease in performance, may be important data which should at the very least be observed and investigated if there are continuing concerns.

An important part of any kind of workplace violence prevention program includes the tenet that managers need to know their employees and not ignore aberrant behaviors.

"We just want to get rid of him."
Hasty Terminations

If avoidance and denial represent the most common errors committed in the area of workplace violence, then the second most common mistake is acting too hastily or prematurely when the decision is finally made to respond.

This rush to action has particularly detrimental consequences in the case of employment terminations. I often receive calls that my services are needed immediately because a potentially dangerous employee is to be terminated, sometimes within a matter of hours (or even minutes). I am asked to either be on site to help manage the situation, or to advise the managers on the telephone.

When I express my concern that the assessment and planning process requires more time, and ask for a delay, the response is sometimes a very emphatic "No, we are tired of dealing with this guy. We need to get rid of him," with some reference to wanting to make a clear statement to other employees, etc.

As will be discussed in more detail later, termination usually represents the company's final opportunity to interact with that particular employee, to assess the risks, and to enact controls and safeguards with any degree of leverage. Once that employee is terminated, our options to assess, monitor, or manage the individual are reduced considerably, never to return. That terminated, potentially retaliatory employee is out there in an unknown location, making unknown plans. Our only available recourse may be to consider various security or legal measures. As will be discussed in Chapter 6, there is much that we can do in order to ensure a safe termination process.

Careful response planning needs to occur not only during the termination process, but whenever an employee of concern is confronted in an action that he or she may percieve as threatening. Many situations go awry and destabilize because there was insufficient planning, in spite of the fact that there were prior concerns about the individual's possible reactions.

> *There is no substitute for careful planning of any adverse action toward an employee of concern. Terminations in particular may represent our last chance to effectively assess, contain, and control future risks to the company and its employees.*

"This guy just gives me the creeps."
Our Internal Alarm System

We often find (unfortunately in retrospect) that employees have long experienced undefined "gut feelings" about a particular fellow employee. They have concerns that they are often not able to explain in more precise terms, and often rationalize them away as being probably unjustified or irrational—and perhaps this is indeed the case. These ambiguous fears can be unfounded or even based on some kind of individual prejudice.

However, I do believe that all of us can sense certain things about others that perhaps we are unable to intellectualize, and that may even be part of some sort of primitive, intuitive warning system.

These "gut feelings" may or may not mean anything, but they are often worth our attention. This is not to imply that a manager has to respond in some designated manner, because someone's behavior gives us the "heebie jeebies," but these feelings should not be simply dismissed. They should at least be figuritively "filed away." If other evidence begins to surface that may suggest a degree of confirmation of these internal feelings, then a further review may be justified based on the preponderance of concerns.

There have been many actual incidences of workplace violence, in which a subsequent investigation revealed that before the perpetrator began exhibiting identifiable warning signs, there already existed a rather pervasive but unexplainable fear of this individual among the other employees.

If an employee is fearful of another employee, that experience should not be routinely dismissed, even if there is no tangible evidence to suppport these feelings.

"It won't do any good to report it."
When Employees Doubt the Company's Commitment

This statement by an employee speaks volumes. It implies that the employees do not have confidence in their company's commitment to respond appropriately and effectively to the percieved threat.

This employee believes that he or she is on his or her own and must be engaged in self-protection, because of a pattern of inaction by the company in regards to threatening behaviors. There have been multiple high-profile disasterous incidents of workplace violence in which the company's managers were repeatedly warned but failed to respond to ensure the employees' safety. Any effective workplace violence prevention program has to have its employees on board and participating in the process.

The company's employees must believe that their employer is serious about the issue of workplace violence, is committed to their well-being, and will effectively respond to their concerns.

"I don't want to get in trouble."
The Employee's Fear of Retaliation

This statement by an employee reflects concerns about confidentiality. He or she ultimately may fear either retribution by the employee of concern or by other empoyees who may consider him or her a "snitch."

Again, for any workplace violence prevention program to be effective, the employees must believe that the system involves a fair, confidential, and careful process that is designed to protect its employees, particularly those who report their concerns. The employees must understand and believe that it will be a confidential process that will consider their safety and other relevant issues, and not act in a hasty, ill-considered fashion.

Employees must trust that the company will handle all complaints in a careful and confidential manner, and will consider the safety and needs of the reporting employee when deciding on a course of action.

"*I didn't know who to call.*"
Defining the Reporting Process

This statement suggests that the employee is not aware of a primary aspect of the company's workplace violence policy: the reporting process.

The core of any violence prevention program is a very clear and consistent message to all the employees, in regards to the chain of communication. It matters less whether the employees report their concerns to their supervisor, human resources, security, or a hotline. What matters is that the employees *know* who is the designated recipient of their report, and that this recipient in turn understands his or her obligations.

It is not sufficient to simply include this information as part of the workplace violence policy; it needs to be disseminated to the employees through a variety of channels. Incidents of workplace violence or threats can occur quickly, without warning, and relatively infrequently. The employees therefore must *know* without question the reporting process, so that they can respond without hesitation.

The company must effectively communicate and remind their employees their respective responsibilities if they encounter a potential threat of violence, which includes a clearly defined reporting system.

"She said that she was afraid of him."
Domestic Abuse as a Workplace Issue

Historically, we have been taught to keep out of each other's personal affairs. In the workplace, that means that we do not comment or attend to anything about another employee's personal life unless we are invited to do so. However, we are discovering that a very significant percentage of workplace violence involves domestic issues.

According to the U.S. Department of Labor, "...almost *three-quarters* of employed battered women reported being harassed by their abusive partners *while at work* and more than half reported missing three days of work each month because of abuse."[2] In another study of domestic violence victims, *96 percent* of those employed had some type of problem in the workplace as a direct result of their abuse or abuser.[3] If you will recall from Chapter 1, we reported that the number one cause of death in the workplace for women is murder. It turns out that over *40%* of these women were murdered by an intimate friend or partner![4] Finally, the Bureau of National Affairs estimates that domestic violence costs $3 to $5 billion annually in security, productivity, turnover, healthcare expenses, and absenteeism.[5] Based on these figures, we clearly can no longer ignore the issue of domestic violence as non-work-related and as outside our concerns.

Incidents of domestic violence can be more particularly devastating. These incidents often catch us by surprise, with an ex-spouse, boyfriend, or girlfriend bursting their way into the workplace with a weapon, enraged with an intent to harm. Needless to say, the person's partner may not become the only victim. These are acts of passion that are beyond anyone's control, once they intrude upon the workplace.

It is not surprising that so much domestic conflict spills over into the workplace. The abused spouse may be in hiding, living with relatives or friends. Her enraged and abusive partner may not know where she lives, sleeps, shops, or dines, but *he knows where she works*! Further, he knows when she arrives at work, where she parks, and through which door she enters. He may even know the location of her desk.

The extent and consequences of domestic violence in the workplace have forced us to rethink our obligatons. Our experience, which is supported statistically, suggests that employees have an obligation not only to report concerns regarding workplace-related behaviors, but also concerns about potential personal issues that may intrude upon the workplace.

On reviewing an incident of domestic-related workplace violence, we often find in retrospect that coworkers had indeed noticed signs of abuse or had overheard phone conversations that have concerned them. These were considered "personal issues" but probably should have been reported in a confidential and discreet manner. There are numerous ways that the company can confront this issue, and certainly it must be accomplished in a confidential and respectful manner.

> *To effectively prevent workplace violence, the company has an obligation to also address any outside relationships that may threaten the safety of the workplace, even if it involves the personal lives of its employees.*

"We don't have those kind of problems here."
Ignorance is Bliss (and Dangerous)

When a manager makes this kind of statement, it generally has the opposite of its intended effect. It should assure the listener that denial is afoot and that there exist some probably very significant problems within this work environment. This statement alone speaks volumes about a culture of denial that is probably pervasive throughout the organization. It assures us that much is not being noticed and that the workplace will be ill-prepared if an act of vioence does surface.

As reported in the first chapter of this book, workplace violence has risen significantly in our society, and no one seems to be immune. This phenomenon has been quite widely distributed across different types of organizations and across different levels within the organization.

How many times have we heard someone being interviewed on the nightly news, with a comment such as "Those kinds of things just don't normally happen in our neighborhood/ town/ company"—usually immediately following a rather horrific incident of violence.

> *Violence can occur in any organization and at any level. To assume otherwise leaves the organization unprepared and more vulnerable.*

The above phrases represent some of what I and other professionals in this field commonly hear when investigating reported threats or incidents of workplace violence. Each of them presents a lesson and presents us with a pattern that is worth investigating and which could point us to possible solutions. In the next chapter, we will discuss the basic steps of preventing workplace violence, based on what can be learned from these patterns.

Endnotes

[1] *Jerner v. Allstate Insurance Co.,* No. 93-0-9472 (Florida Circuit Court, 1995).

[2] New York Victim Services Agency Report on the Costs of Domestic Violence, 1987, as reported in "Facts on Working Women," Women's Bureau, U.S. Department of Labor, October 1996.

[3] "Domestic Violence: An Occupational Impact Study," Domestic Violence Intervention Services, Inc., Tulsa, Oklahoma, July 27, 1992, as reported in "Facts on Working Women," Women's Bureau, U.S. Department of Labor, October 1996.

[4] Government Executive, December 1996.

[5] J. Snyder, "Domestic Abuse Affects Job, Too," *The Honolulu Advertiser*, November 3, 2003.

Chapter 4

Preventing Workplace Violence
A Ten-Step Solution

In Chapter 1, we began with the assumption that workplace violence, in spite of alarming statistics that may suggest otherwise, does not have to happen—that it is a *preventable event.* This chapter will present and discuss the ten essential and specific steps that will ensure that assumption—steps that will hopefully be more obvious, based on the experiences summarized in this and the previous chapter.

---

10 Steps
To Prevent Workplace Violence

1. Establish Effective Pre-employment Screening Procedures
2. Compose a Workplace Violence Policy
3. Promote Employee Awareness
4. Maintain Workplace Violence Training Programs
5. Develop a Threat Response Process

---

6. Review the Disciplinary, Grievance, and Termination Procedures
7. Utilize Employee Assistance Programs
8. Refer to Outplacement Services
9. Train Supervisory and Conflict Resolution Skills
10. Identify External Resources

1. Pre-Employment Screening

As we have previously noted, there are individuals who may be predisposed to violence and who may actually have a history that supports that. A fundamental cornerstone of effective prevention is to not allow these individuals into your workplace to begin with.

A good, careful process of pre-employment screening is critical. While this is obvious, many companies fail to follow even their own established procedures. As discussed, there are many reasons for unwise haste in this endeavor, but the time spent in careful investigation and discussion is time well-spent, as the costs of hiring a potentially dangerous individual can be devastating. Even without the costs specifically related to aggressive behaviors, retaining and eventually discharging problem employees always stresses the company's resources in a variety of ways.

As noted earlier, it is relatively easy to ignore or to not seek out critical data when hiring, as there are pressures operating to complete the process quickly. Also, we all have a natural tendency to begin to analyze data before we have accumulated all of it. This is not exactly a negative characteristic, but it can be problematic if it leads to a kind of myopia, in which we then selectively attend only to data that validates our preconceived (and often preferred) opinion.

There is another reason to make certain that the company engages in a sound hiring process: the company could be found liable if an employee engages in behavior that would have been predictable if it had investigated his history more carefully when initially hired. A court, for example, awarded an employee of Avis Rent A Car $750,000 after she was raped by a coworker. It turned out that this coworker had lied on his original application, and actually was serving a three-year prison sentence on a robbery conviction during the time that he reported on his application form that he was in college. The company was found negligent in that it did not sufficiently check the information on the application.[1]

Unfortunately, verification of information at application is important, as evidenced by the results of recent surveys that indicate that from *25% to 40%* of job applicants lie about, embellish, or conceal their qualifications or backgrounds on job applications.[2] According to a 1998 Society for Human Resource Management survey, most employers have discovered falsified information during reference checks.[3] If an employer discovers that an applicant has lied about one issue, it should be assumed that they he or she has probably lied about other issues, too.

Contacting references

Contacting prior employers is always critical, and it is recognized here that many employers typically only provide dates of employment or certain standard responses, in order to protect themselves legally. However, there are some leading questions that the interviewer can sometimes pose that may allow that reference somehow to alert the interviewer to potential problems without feeling compromised. Oftentimes, the interviewer neglects to ask critical questions, due to an assumption that he or she will not be able to obtain the necessary information anyway. It never hurts to ask! It is also advisable, if at all possible, to speak to that individual's supervisor (or someone with firsthand knowledge of the applicant), as opposed to just going through their personnel or human resource managers.

It is also critical that we not ask questions of the references in a manner that suggests we are attempting to affirm a previously held opinion. For example, calling someone and saying, "I assume this employee caused no difficulty, right?" is an invitation to the other individual to be agreeable, and very clearly implies that you want the person to answer in a certain manner. Sometimes, we may actually pose a question, such that the other party only has to concur with and reinforce our obviously held opinion— an opinion that may be motivated by our desire to successfully expedite the hiring process. The former employer is let off the hook and does not have to formulate a response that leaves him or her more accountable. I advise that the interviewer ask open-ended questions and wait patiently for an answer, resisting the temptation to answer for the interviewee, especially if he or she appears to be struggling with the answer. This also applies when interviewing applicants.

Sometimes, references other than former employers are ignored or not sufficiently questioned, as we assume that anyone listed voluntarily as a personal reference will provide a positive opinion. Remarkably, we have actually telephoned references of existing employees as part of our data collection process, who have in turn provided very negative comments about the applicant. And these were references that the employee him- or herself had volunteered in the original application, who were reportedly contacted before the applicant was hired!

Interviewing the applicant

Carefully reviewing an applicant's history, with an eye to anything that suggests problems, can suggest critical follow-up questions and further investigation. Oftentimes, when we review someone's application for employment, we can sometimes "read between the lines." It is important to take the time to carefully review with the applicant any perceived gaps, inconsistencies, or insufficient responses in his or her history or explanations. Ask applicants to explain all periods of unemployment. Explain to the applicant the consequences of falsification *or* omission of critical information.

All potential employees ought to undergo an interview process. If possible, more than one interview should be conducted, and by different interviewers. Open-ended questions should be included that address past areas of conflict with their employers, their relationships with supervisors and coworkers, and examples of how they handled past stressful situations within the workplace. Specific questions can be devised that ask them to comment on critical areas of concern, such as how they express their anger, resolve conflicts and handle pressure. The questions can be not only open-ended, but can be stated in such a way that it reduces the chance that the individual can easily deflect the issue. For example, instead of asking whether the applicant intimidates others, the interviewer's question can be, "Tell me the ways in which you may intimidate people." Asking about any experiences in which an applicant believed that he or she was unfairly treated in the workplace can yield valuable data, which can be followed up with further questioning.

Many employers have found that contracting the services of a psychological consultant specializing in personnel selection is useful and cost-effective, given the relative cost of even one "bad hire." Even if the company cannot afford this service, I recommend that the hiring process involve a conferencing between two or more managers, so that they can act as reality checks for each other. Conferring with a colleague always helps the manager surface concerns and obtain feedback regarding the legitimacy of these concerns. The process of expressing his or her concerns alone may be sufficient to help the manager recognize any doubts, even if his or her colleague acts only as a sounding board.

Background investigation

Utilizing criminal background checks is *always* cost-effective. Those with criminal histories are not likely to acknowledge this history when asked, unless they know that the company will be conducting a background check. These need to be as extensive and as comprehensive as is legally and financially allowable.

Companies should consult with their attorneys as to what they can or cannot address in the hiring process, and should utilize resources available to them. One incident of workplace violence will be more costly than all of the costs in time and finances that the company spends when conducting a careful selection process. While under some legal restraints as to what data they can obtain, organizations may at the same time be considered negligent if they hire a dangerous employee without an appropriate investigation during the application process. For more information on the reference checking process, refer to Wendy Bliss' 2001 guidebook on this subject. (See Bibliography for details.)

As a final note, the separation process is difficult, hazardous, and costly, and it generally cannot occur without undergoing a sometimes drawn-out established process. It is therefore imperative that the company acts as quickly as possible whenever it becomes obvious that an employee is not fitting into the organization or is representing a potential risk. The longer that individual continues to be embedded in the organization and the longer his or her behaviors continue to be reinforced through response avoidance, the more difficult the separation.

2. The Workplace Violence Policy

It is imperative for any company not only to have, but also to loudly commit itself to, a clear, established policy on aggression and violence in the workplace. This policy should make clear, in unequivocal terms, the company's position in regards to any threats or aggressive acts that may imperil the safety of its employees and customers.

The policy provides the foundation of the company's Workplace Violence Prevention and Response Program. It serves to communicate to its employees the company's commitment to an aggression-free workplace, and should do so without ambivalence or ambiguity. This policy will not, in and of itself, reduce aggressive behavior, but it lays a necessary foundation for all subsequent decisions. However, if the policy is written and *communicated* in a manner that leaves no question about the company's commitment, it may also serve to alter the organizational culture, such that it will help to contain those employees with impulse- and anger-management problems.

A policy does not have to be that specific. There is no

standard, and there are a variety of models that are utilized by different companies. Policies generally are best if kept simple and relatively brief, with the details of implementation addressed in other documents and during the company's training programs. (See Appendix A for an example of a workplace violence policy.)

Workplace violence policies *at the minimum* should include the following four general issues:

1. A general statement of the company's position.

This statement should reflect the company's clear commitment to a violence-free workplace and should be unequivocal. It communicates to its employees that the organization is assuming a *proactive* approach that cares about the safety of its people. It should ideally imply a philosophy that the company embraces the highest standard of behavior for itself and expects that of all its employees—that it holds itself accountable at all levels of the organization.

Be cautious when using the term "zero tolerance." This is an effective term if it is used to describe the company's total commitment to an aggression-free workplace, but it may also imply a very restrictive, inflexible (and often harsh) response. The policy should not unnecessarily tie the hands of those having to respond to the myriad of situations that may be defined as threatening behavior. Most importantly, the company does not want to discourage reporting or early intervention, because of the employees' fear that management will over-respond in an inflexible and harsh manner when they report their concerns. One of the cornerstones of an effective workplace violence program is that the employees believe that the company will respond in a reasonable and fair manner. The company does not want to imply by "zero tolerance" that it will respond to each and every incident with maximum punishment (i.e. termination), but it does want to communicate that it will respond *each and every time*.

2. A definition of violence that is general and not overly restrictive.

We earlier defined aggression and violence for our purposes as *any kind of conduct that is intimidating, hostile, offensive, or threatening.* This can occur as (but is not limited to) verbal threats, written statements, physical contact, or threatening gestures. Any attempt to harm can be assumed under the definition of aggression and violence. It can include harassment, unwanted pursuit (i.e., stalking), and a variety of psychological aggressive or emotionally abusive acts, such as bullying, verbal humiliation, and public ridicule. An act of violence may also be represented by even more passive-aggressive forms, such as spreading rumors, withholding critical information, silent phone calls, etc. It should include incidents from inside and outside the workplace.

The policy's definition of aggressive behavior is up to the individual company and to what standard it wants to commit. I generally recommend a very broad definition of violence, with an array of examples, but which also cautions that these examples do not represent an exhaustive list. No list can cover all the possible manifestations of inappropriate or aggressive conduct that can occur in the context of human relations. However, some companies may want to target particular behaviors that they consider critical in their particular environment. I have seen policies, for example, that have restricted "discriminatory remarks that cause discomfort," "menacing gestures," "derogatory statements," or even simply "profanity." Some have explicitly included suicidal threats.

The company does not want to overly restrict itself and risk discouraging a reporting of aggression for fear that it does not fit a narrow definition. The company has to communicate to its employees through this document and through subsequent communications that it is interested in hearing from its employees on matters beyond the stereotypic gun-wielding assailant. Furthermore, the company wants to communicate to its employees that it is the *employees'* responsibility to report *any* situation that is of concern. Whether that behavior actually constitutes a violation of the policy is a decision made by those who are trained to conduct a careful, professional, and respectable investigation process.

3. The expectations of both managers and general employees.

As with most of the policy, this does not have to be a lengthy section, but there should be a clear statement of the company's expectations of the behavior of its employees. This includes an affirmation that the company expects its employees to refrain from the defined behaviors, but it should also include what is expected of each employee when they have knowledge of actions or statements that may represent a risk. When discussing the reporting process, the policy may also do well to reinforce the company's commitment to the safety, confidentiality, and protection from retaliation for the reporters.

The organization would, in most cases, restrict employees from carrying of any kind of weapons in the workplace, either on their person, anywhere on the physical premises, or in any vehicle brought onto the premises.

Those in supervisory roles are often further expected to be responsible for the behaviors of others, and to maintain sufficient awareness, so that they can effectively and proactively respond to any perceived act of aggression. A discussion of a manager's obligations may include a reference to his or her role in the prevention and the subsequent evaluation process. Further, it may address managers' responsibilities when having to investigate, report, and document reported incidents.

This section may also outline or even detail the company's crisis response process, along with an identification of those in charge of the response process, and a description of their respective duties. Again, too much detail in a policy statement is not generally recommended, so as not to unnecessarily restrict the range of responses that may be required in all of the situations that may be reported.

4. An elucidation of the reporting and overall communication process.

This may be the most important part of the policy. As we have seen, denial and avoidance are the easiest responses, and employees have many psychological and even practical reasons to avoid reporting their concerns. The employees have to be provided an easy, safe, and clearly articulated reporting process that can help override their resistance. This communication process has to be workable within the company's existing culture and structure. Furthermore, all participants in this process need to be aware of their respective roles, as will be discussed in the section on training.

Each company must consider this part of the policy carefully, because this forms the basis of some of the guidelines that will be communicated to the employees. The organization needs to ask itself whether this proposed reporting process will actually work within its unique environment and culture. Are there any gaps in this reporting process? Is there any possibility that information will not move along this chain effectively? The reporting process has to be one the employees will be willing to use. Some companies, for example, have included a confidential "hotline" as an option. Some have employees report their concerns to supervisors, others to human resources, or even directly to corporate security. It matters less how or to whom the information is reported than the clarity with which it is communicated and understood (and accepted) by the employees.

It may be useful to have representatives from different segments of the employee base (i.e. front-line workers, supervisors, Human Resources, Security, etc.) review and provide input regarding the applicability of the policy before implementation. As with any critical document of this nature, the company should have the policy reviewed by corporate legal counsel.

3. Promoting Employee Involvement

It is not sufficient to simply compose and announce a policy on workplace violence. Even sending out written notification to all employees and having them sign agreements may not be sufficient to break through an existing climate of denial. Just because the upper levels of the organization have decided to institute a new effective workplace violence policy does not mean that the employees will automatically be on board. And as stated previously, even the most perfectly constructed workplace violence program will ultimately be relatively ineffective without the support of the employees.

The company needs to conduct an active campaign to promote and encourage employee *participation.* Including them in the process at the very beginning, by having representatives provide input about the policy or by circulating surveys to make sure their concerns are addressed, is a way to accomplish that. At some level and through some means, the company needs to communicate its commitment, and that the company holds *every* employee accountable to a certain standard of behavior.

In the end, the employees must believe that they are an integral part of this system and that it is to their benefit to participate. If the employee population feels that this is in place to protect them, and that it will be administered in a fair and confidential manner, they are much more likely to become part of this process. The company must somehow communicate that this policy is because the company *cares* for the safety of each and every employee, and this has to be believable. The communication must address some of the reasons for employee resistance that may be embedded in that particular culture or that may have been discovered in the early stages of the assessment process.

There are different ways the organization can accomplish this, some dependent on the structure and culture of the organization. Much of this can be accomplished through employee awareness programs that will be discussed in the next section. These programs may have to be provided on a periodic basis to remind employees of their responsibilities. Managers must first be made aware of this policy and know how to address any concerns that may be expressed by their subordinates.

All of this obviously occurs within an existing culture. If the organization creates and maintains an atmosphere that promotes respect and open communication, then employees will naturally feel a part of the process and will be more participatory and less resistant.

4. Employee Training Programs

All employees should undergo some kind of educational program that makes certain that they are aware of their respective duties and obligations under the company's workplace violence program. The level and the nature of training will vary significantly, generally along four different groups. The content of the training is progressive, in that each group mentioned below generally receives the same training as the prior group, with the addition of skills and information that is unique to their role.

a. *General Employees.* Training for the general employee population can be relatively brief and can be delivered though a variety of forms of communication. The goals are primarily to promote employee awareness of the many manifestations of violent behaviors, explain the company's policy regarding this issue, and define the employees' respective responsibilities under this policy. Further, significant time could be spent on increasing awareness of the early warning signs—the antecedents of potential violence. As discussed, the understanding and the cooperation of the company's employees form the cornerstone of an effective program. The message delivered should inspire confidence in the commitment and the ability of management to address this issue effectively, confidentially, and respectfully, once the employee does come forward with a concern. Above all, the employees must understand that the safety of themselves and their coworkers is completely reliant on their willingness to report significant events. They truly represent the company's front line of defense. The training would ideally be participatory and address the specifics of their unique workplace context.

b. *Supervisors.* Once an employee reports an incident or concern to his or her supervisor, the supervisor in turn needs to know what he or she is to do with that information. The company needs to be clear in explaining to those who manage others the exact nature of their responsibilities. Under most workplace violence programs, they have to respond in some fashion, but are generally not expected to take full responsibility for investigating or responding to the issue without alerting others within the organization who are more specifically trained. If supervisors are expected to first investigate, or if they have some latitude in terms of their response or decision to report, then this will generally require more detailed training. For example, if they are not to report all concerns about potential violence, then the trainers need to clarify what is and is not considered reportable, based on the company's program. Managers certainly would require more extensive training in the awareness and recognition of the signs and symptoms of individuals who are potentially at risk. A supervisor plays a critical role in any effective violence prevention program in his or her ability to recognize when an individual employee is in trouble or under significant stress. In our workshops for supervisors and managers, we also typically include training on the basic techniques of de-escalation and conflict resolution.

c. *Critical Personnel.* This category generally includes those within human resources, corporate security, or anyone who may be more likely to be involved in the decision-making process in critical situations. While this training includes what is provided above to other employees, it may also cover an overview of the threat assessment, response, and management process. It typically may include, for example, how to engage or not engage the "disgruntled" or problem employee when various employee actions are required, such as discipline or termination. Most importantly, it trains these personnel on recognizing and identifying those situations that may require more specialized intervention from either internal or external resources. This can also include more in-depth training on how to safely manage conflict or contain potentially hazardous situations until further help can arrive.

d. *Threat Response Personnel.* This is the most comprehensive level of training. It is recommended that the company have designated personnel who are specifically assigned the responsibility for coordinating and managing the company's investigation and response to reported threats. This individual or team (preferably) has to develop and oversee the workings of the company's threat response program. While no team or individual is generally expected to know everything about the process of threat assessment and management, they are the ones who will have to call on outside advice and resources when needed. These personnel have the responsibility to make certain that the process is managed effectively. They must therefore understand their obligations under the company's response plan, understand how to carry out investigations, and be aware of the various response options that may be available. These employees will have to be trained to understand the basic response demands of a wide range of scenarios. They may need, for example, to understand the basis of post-incident debriefing, or even how to manage the media after a high-profile event. Again, these employees are not expected to be threat response experts. (After all, it is presumed that they have other jobs within the organization.) They do, however, need to be aware of the range of possible responses and the range of resources, particularly external specialists, who may be available and can be called on when needed. The formation and content of the company's Threat Response Team will be covered in the next chapter.

5. A Threat Response Plan

A Threat Response Plan is usually the step that follows policy development. However, this generally has to await the designation and training of a Threat Response Team, as it is often this team who generally takes responsibility for developing this plan, since they are the ones responsible for making it work. A plan, with a documented process, is critical, since the explosive chain of events that are confronted by this team often do not allow much time for confusion or indecision.

The first task for the team is to complete an assessment and review of the needs of their particular organization. This team should have an understanding of the unique set of risks that their organization is likely to confront. This will include an analysis of the company's current ability to respond to threats and violent incidents, along with a review of past episodes, to determine how effectively they were managed. This team is not only responsible for formulating the response plan, but generally oversees all aspects of the prevention program, in order to reduce identified risks within the organization.

The plan should contain a description of the general protocol that the team follows whenever it receives a report, along with an outline of the response and documentation process. This protocol should include clarification of how and by whom the report is received, and should define the responsibilities of each member within the process. Not everyone in the team may be involved in every reported incident, for example.

The plan would ideally be incorporated into a manual that covers all aspects of the assessment and response process, which can be utilized when training future team members. This plan needs to be periodically reviewed, as does the entire workplace violence program, to assure its effectiveness and that it continues to address the goals of the organization. The reporting and communication process should be reviewed, such that any gaps in the system can be rectified.

The response plan's manual should include all information relevant to the many needs of an organization that could find itself in the middle of a potentially explosive situation, including all the contact information for critical specialists and resources. As will be addressed in the above-mentioned training process, there should be an understanding of when outside agencies are called—agencies such as the local police, threat assessment specialists, legal counsel, and security consultants, to mention a few.

The plan should also include a documentation and review process, so that the team, when debriefing after each case, can analyze their work and address any deficiencies that may have been noted. This review is critical in order to ensure the credibility of the process. If a reported incident is mishandled in any manner (i.e. an informant's confidentiality is compromised), then word may spread within the company, sowing doubts about the program's effectiveness.

There are many issues that a threat response plan may have to address, from the details of the investigation process to post-incident press releases. Each company must develop a plan that is specific to the needs and goals and culture of its particular organization.

6. Grievance, Disciplinary, and Termination Processes

My experience suggests that most violence between employees, by a large margin, occurs either after an adverse employment action or after the occurrence of an internal event that represents a longstanding issue or grievance. That is not to say that these actions or events *caused* the violence or even were a major contributing factor in many cases. However, the final event that *triggers* an act of violence by an at-risk employee is typically an event that occurs within the organization, generally an action toward that employee.

Grievances

A secondary but critical role of any effective disciplinary or grievance process should be to aid in the early detection of potential problems. Many incidents of workplace violence are perpetrated by individuals who have a history of grievances but who believe that their grievances were not adequately addressed by management. Oftentimes, these are the "disgruntled employees" who feel that they have been traumatized by the actions of managers or coworkers to some degree and that their concerns about this stressor have gone largely ignored.

The company needs to be aware of and address grievances presented by employees, even if the complaints do not appear legitimate or justifiable. If these complaints continue in an unrelenting manner or if they are not considered reasonable, the company may need to engage that employee in an assessment process, in order to ensure that he or she does not represent some kind of risk. Even if the employee does not appear to represent a risk of harm, a disgruntled or agitated employee will cost the company in a myriad of ways. Engaging that employee in some kind of interactive process may uncover some areas that are available to resolution, and will at the very least meet that employee's need for acknowledgment.

Discipline

Disciplinary policy may require review to make certain that it is workable, enforceable, and consistently applied. The greatest mistake that many companies make is not applying their already-established disciplinary procedures in a consistent and equitable manner. Oftentimes, discipline is ignored completely until the behavior has become so consistent and so obnoxious that there is a tendency to jump to a higher level of discipline, such that it destabilizes the situation and inflames the individual.

We have already discussed this in terms of a company's

avoidance of bullying or intimidating employees. Few of us enjoy confrontation, and many managers would like to err on the side of the employee by "giving him a break." Empathy for the employee is noble and often a sign of good management, but more often than not, this refusal to discipline more accurately represents simple avoidance in these instances. Even if the manager believes that there are extenuating circumstances and that the usual disciplinary action would be too harsh, the employee should still be confronted about his or her behavior, and the decision regarding the company's action documented, with the reasons for that action. This documentation helps to ensure that the manager acts in an accountable manner, and is not simply ignoring the issue.

The role of discipline is not just punitive; its primary benefit in most instances is both educational and preventative. A disciplinary response serves to remind the employees of the company's policies and the company's commitment to those policies. It reminds the employee that he or she can count on the company to be consistent and *responsible*—that is, to *respond*—and not ignore violations for any reason. Members of an organization often determine what is permissible behavior by the response received when someone engages in that behavior, not by a written policy or law. Therefore, disciplinary action— especially when it is consistently applied—sends a message both to the member receiving the discipline and to the rest of the organization, which will act to effectively reduce the incidence of those behaviors by everyone.

Employee termination

The termination process is critical when an employee is believed to be at risk for violence. This is particularly important, since the company usually forfeits any means of influencing or monitoring that employee once he or she exits. Due to this and other reasons, the termination process should be carefully considered and planned *before* the termination. More often than not, companies wait until after the employee is fired before assessing the risk and making safety-related decisions. This is an important enough topic to have its own chapter, and will be discussed in detail in Chapter 6.

Other adverse actions

There are other critical periods that will occur in the lifespan of an organization, in which an employee's status is adversely affected. Whenever a company is undergoing any kind of significant change in which its employees' jobs or lifestyles are affected, a careful review process is recommended. This process should review the action, the manner in which it is carried out, and its impact on individual employees, even those indirectly affected. For example, large layoffs not only affect separated employees, but also may have some impact on those who remain.

Further, a company needs to not only identify potential inflammatory issues, but also identify those particular employees about whom they have concerns. These may be employees who will suffer substantial or atypical loses due to this action, because of certain situational or personal issues; or these can be employees who may, for one reason or another, be considered at risk for retaliatory or aggressive behavior. In these instances, the company may decide to engage its threat response team to investigate, and propose a plan of approach that will safeguard the company's employees during the process.

7. Employee Assistance Programs

If an employee is experiencing emotional stress beyond what his or her existing resources can effectively manage, that employee becomes at risk for a multitude of subsequent problems, many of which may manifest themselves within the workplace. While this stress may not be initially related to workplace events, it will more than likely affect the employee's performance and relationships within the workplace in some capacity, if the issues are not resolved.

While it can be argued that it is not the organization's role to assist its employees with their personal problems, it is generally considered cost-effective to provide employees with basic resources to help resolve the crises in their lives, as a preventive measure. Many issues are most easily resolvable in the early stages, and if addressed early, are less likely to escalate to dangerous levels or adversely affect the company.

Even if early and short-term intervention cannot resolve the employee's problems, there is certainly an advantage to having a mental health professional involved who can refer the employee to other resources, or who can hopefully identify the existence of more serious issues. At the least, the employee will have access to a professional counselor who can advise him or her and take precautionary action if the employee appears to represent a risk to others.

Every company should consider using some kind of referral or assistance program, in which employees who are experiencing significant stress can obtain relatively easy access to mental health or substance abuse treatment when needed. Employee Assistance Programs (EAPs) in particular have proven to be a very effective resource for many companies. EAPs and other such programs are there to help the employees with their identified needs, which can in turn reduce the potential for violent behavior. As noted previously, however, the EAP cannot function simply as a single solution or depository for problem employees, but it can serve as a useful resource that will ultimately reduce aggressive responses to stress and help identify those who may be at risk.

8. Outplacement Services

The risks posed by a separated employee are almost always reduced (if not eliminated) when that employee finds work elsewhere. Being able to refer the employee to a resource that can help him or her locate or prepare for another job will benefit that employee, help to protect the company, and in the long run, benefit the rest of society—as there will be one less disgruntled, unemployed individual in need of support. If nothing else, providing this kind of benefit to someone who is no longer in the organization sends a clear message that the organization is aware of and concerned about the effects of its decision on the employee's life.

Outplacement programs can provide a range of services. Some may offer access to databases regarding available jobs; others include offices and needed equipment such as computers; and still others may include support groups, coaching, or educational programs. At the very least, this kind of assistance program can provide structure and guidance to out-of-work individuals who find themselves isolated by suddenly having a significant portion of their life taken from them. It also can potentially provide relationships and a means of emotional support. The outplacement counselors cannot offer psychotherapy, but can identify potential emotional problems and make the appropriate referrals.

Many organizations actually have the outplacement counselor meet with the individual at the workplace immediately after the termination meeting. This is often preferred, as it is sometimes difficult for the ex-employee to initiate that contact, as he or she may not be able to appreciate how this can be of help, especially during the depressing and confusing post-termination period. If the company is concerned that the ex-employee presents a potential risk, the outplacement counselor can serve as another source of information, as part of the company's ongoing monitoring process.

9. Training Supervisory & Conflict Resolution Skills

As mentioned above, the triggering event for workplace violence is often an adverse employment action. Many times, however, the event that traumatized the employee and triggered that particular reaction was not what the manager said or did, but *how* it was said or done. The triggering event is often a comment or action from a supervisor that was, in retrospect, inconsiderate or at least inappropriate in light of the employee's history or circumstances.

The organization is responsible for bad supervisors and needs to make certain that those individuals who are supervising others have the basic skills to do so. The long-term costs of abusive or intimidating supervisors far outweigh any short-term gain, in terms of discipline or productivity. Sometimes, supervisors can make inappropriate remarks simply because they are unaware of issues that may be critical for a particular employee. Sometimes they may not be aware of the emotional stress that a particular employee is under, and may make a comment or place a demand that triggers a response—a response that could have been anticipated if the supervisor had taken the time to *know his workers.* As noted under the section on training, supervisors need to understand the basic signs and symptoms of a troubled employee, and should be aware of the available resources.

Supervisors would benefit from any kind of training that would increase their ability to interact with their employees in a more positive manner. Active listening skills, basic conflict management techniques, and positive approaches to discipline and performance reviews are all skills that generally have to be taught. Anyone who manages others has to be able to suspend his or her natural reactions to stressful or confrontational events and remain the voice of reason and reassurance. Few, if any of us are born with those skills.

Many companies are now teaching their managers—and sometimes all their employees—basic conflict and crisis management skills. Some organizations are establishing specific dispute resolution programs, in order to respond to and address potentially costly conflict in the early stages. This is *always* cost-effective in my experience. Conflict is inevitable in all human relationships and within all organizations, and many situations that have exploded into costly incidents of violence have included a history of unresolved conflict. Further, we now understand enough about this area to know what works, and we also know that these skills are trainable, with significant benefits.

As previously noted, maintaining a general culture of respect and open communication will automatically serve to reduce risk. The management style of the supervisors will reflect how successful the company has been in promoting and fostering that culture.

10. Utilizing Outside Resources

No organization can by itself prevent or control workplace violence. There are too many specialized skills that may be required in the assessment, prevention, and management process. As I will continue to emphasize throughout this volume, these events are not easily manageable. They often require a creative solution process and sometimes a reliance on many resources, as there is no single formula.

Outside resources may include law enforcement, local community and mental health services, public social services, substance abuse clinics, outplacement counseling, psychological evaluators, security consultants, and threat assessment consultants, among others. Having a relationship with these and other agencies can be immensely valuable, and it allows the company to get back to its work.

Every company in this day and age needs to review its physical security and make certain that it has protective measures in place. Technology in this area is a rapidly expanding field. Access control, alarm systems, parking lot security, and such can be critical issues that may require the services of a security consultant. Likewise, a threat assessment professional—a relatively recent area of specialization that is further discussed in the next chapter—can provide critical assessment and intervention services in potentially high-risk situations.

Any referral to an outside resource is completed as part of the company's overall response plan and cannot be considered as a way to somehow shift responsibility. While the organization may utilize the services of outside resources, the company still has to oversee the process, in order to safeguard its interests and maintain safety for its employees.

In this chapter, we have focused on *primary* prevention—the procedures that will help the organization detect and resolve potential risks *before* they have a chance to truly threaten the organization. The success of any violence prevention program is measured not only by a reduction of incidents, but by how effectively the organization responds to those potentially high-risk incidents that will inevitably arise. In the following chapter, we will focus on what to do when the organization faces a threat of violence that requires an immediate response.

_____

Endnotes

[1] As reported by Steve Kauper, "Corporate Liability: Sharing the Blame for Workplace Violence" at www.noworkviolence.com.
[2] W. Bliss, *Legal, Effective References.* (Alexandria, VA: Society for Human Resource Management, 2001).
[3] Ibid.

Chapter 5

Responding to a Threat
An Overview of the
Assessment and Management Process

What Constitutes a "Threat?"

One of the more alarming situations that any company has to encounter occurs when there is a reported *threat of violence*, as it is often termed in the literature. When we refer to a "threat of violence," there is often an assumption that this term is limited to direct statements that one individual explicitly delivers to another—a statement that would be clearly perceived by anyone as representing intent to harm. In actuality, the term "threat," is utilized in this context as *any manner of action or behavior or remark that suggests that someone is at risk of harming himself or others*. These threats are actually rarely presented in a direct, verbalized manner, and as often as not, may be ambiguous and open to interpretation, sometimes by design.

So what actually represents a threat? People experience a "threat" in a multitude of ways, some of them unique. When it involves a verbal statement, it can be ambiguous and suggestive, ranging from, "You will be sorry you said that" to "I'll be back." A threat does not have to be spoken, and even if verbalized, it is usually the manner, intonation, gestures, or facial expressions of the presenter that have suggested the presence of a "threat." Further, the statement is generally made within the context of an ongoing conflict or situation, such that it often cannot be fully appreciated outside that context.

Threats can be represented by the most subtle of gestures. There was recently an incident in a small Southern town, in which the threat consisted of the individual "pointing his finger." When we asked these very concerned employees to demonstrate this "threat," they presented a very subtle gesture that could hardly be described even as pointing. However, those who experienced this and were on the receiving end of this act were familiar with this individual and with both the immediate and historical context within which it occurred, such that there was *no question* in their minds of this gentleman's intent. The threat does not have to be verbal, written, or even gestural. The message can occur in many forms and can be symbolic and sometimes purposely ambiguous. A threat can consist of placing a target on someone's door or leaving a bullet on another employee's desk, both of which are examples that have occurred in recent memory.

A threat is very simply *any behavior* that is *reasonably perceived* by the receiving individual as a suggestion that the other individual *intends to harm* him or her. This threat itself is defined as an aggressive act by most workplace violence policies. This may appear to represent a broad definition, but if an employee or anyone else in the workplace believes that they are threatened, it behooves us to investigate and to further understand the context of the situation, in order to determine whether that person's safety is in jeopardy.

A "threat" is any manner of action or behavior or remark that suggests that someone is at risk of harming himself or others.

Types of threats

There are many types of threats, and there certainly can be different motivations behind an issuance of a threat. It may be an *expressive* act, in that it represents an expression of emotion, in which the individual is attempting to express the degree of his or her anger or dissatisfaction. A threat can be *instrumental,* in that it is intended to manipulate or to somehow influence someone's behavior in some manner, or to produce a particular reaction. It may represent an attempt to promote a sense of fear or to otherwise control the behavior or emotions of the victim. It may indeed be *a warning.*

As noted, many threats are *veiled* or *indirect,* and may be so by design. If the victim or others are confused or uncertain as to the nature of the threat, this can serve to essentially empower the threatening party to a certain extent. In essence, it "keeps them guessing," and this uncertainty will, by itself, promote greater anxiety for the victim.

Many threats are what we term *conditional* threats in that the individual is threatening an action *if* something else occurs, which is generally in the category of an instrumental threat. A conditional threat places additional pressure on the situation, which those conducting the assessment should take into account. This may be an individual who has essentially committed him- or herself to a promise and may feel therefore compelled to act on this, in order to maintain an internal sense of integrity.

Many individuals who threaten violence do so in order to regain or maintain a sense of power or control. For those who are managing the situation and attempting to reduce the risk, it is therefore imperative that part of this process includes a consideration of how the subject can maintain that sense of control through other, nonviolent means.

The existence and the content of a particular threat by itself does not tell us much. As noted in previous chapters, threat assessment is not simply an analysis of the threatening individual's characteristics. Likewise, a threat *must be understood within the context* of the one who issued it and the purpose that it serves.

Further, a threat exists within a broader, situational context that needs to be similarly understood, in order for the risks to be adequately managed.

Making vs. posing a threat

Certainly, not all people who make threats carry them out. In fact, it is safe to say that most people who make threats do *not* actually carry them out. Conversely, not all who commit a violent act warn us first. While we are interested in any kind of threatening statement, we are far more interested in hearing about individuals who—for whatever reason—*pose* a threat, as opposed to just those individuals who *make* a threat. In other words, whether someone actually said something or did something that has been determined as a "threat" is less important than if others perceive the person as a threat.

We have responded to many reported threats, in which subsequent investigations have revealed that those who work with this individual have long experienced a vague, indefinable dread or anxiety in their interactions with the subject. They have felt threatened, even without specific identifiable reason. It is often conceivable that they were acting on some sort of cumulative data that may not have been entirely conscious.

If a company receives these kinds of reports, it certainly does not confirm that the individual is indeed dangerous, or even suggest that the organization should respond in any particular manner. In fact, these feelings and reports may be entirely unfounded and/or based on other agendas or prejudices. However, the organization should investigate and arrive at a decision as to whether any kind of action is necessary, as opposed to automatically dismissing them as perhaps groundless or not worthy of review.

The Threat Response Team

The first thing that has to happen when someone reports a potentially threatening set of circumstances is to make certain that this information is quickly and effectively routed to the individual or individuals within the company who are responsible for the company's response. This will be generally spelled out by the company's policy.

Preferably, one individual or a team is responsible for coordinating and planning the company's response to a perceived threat. Almost all of the experts in this field have concurred that the establishment of a "threat response team" (or "risk management team" or "crisis response team") is the most effective vehicle to coordinate and plan this process.

This process truly works better through a multi-disciplinary approach. Utilization of a trained *team* allows for a "meeting of the minds" in which different individuals with different roles within the organization can each analyze the problem from their operational perspective, and can be available to challenge each other's ideas and proposals. We have been involved in many situations in which we have arrived at a relatively well-considered response plan only to discover through a question or insight of one of the team members that we had overlooked a critical variable that would have adversely affected the outcome. This process simply works better when it is a team effort, and generally an interdisciplinary one. These team members will serve as the company's specialists, and should be trained accordingly.

The organization's response team would be ideally responsible for coordinating all aspects of the company's workplace violence program. This would include:

1. Reviewing the organization's policy.
2. Developing a Threat Response Plan.
3. Ensuring that employees, particularly critical personnel, are aware of their respective responsibilities.
4. Establishing and maintaining an effective reporting process.
5. Investigating reported incidents.
6. Managing incidents when and after they occur.
7. Overseeing the company's overall prevention program.

The members of the team may vary. It is typically suggested that the core team consist of representatives from security/risk management, legal, and human resources, but this depends on the organization's structure. Other permanent members may include (but are not limited to) someone from management, a member of the company's occupational health or medical team, and a consulting psychologist who specializes in threat assessment.

It is generally not recommended that a representative from the company's Employee Assistance Program (EAP) serve as a member of this team. Employees must view EAPs as a confidential resource, and the organization therefore should not jeopardize the credibility of that program. The organization's goals would generally be better served if the EAP remains as a potential option, as part of the resulting management plan.

In order to function adequately, this team should undergo a training process, as proposed in the last chapter, in order to clarify their roles, understand the threat response process, and discuss response options. Generally, it is the team's responsibility to review the company's policy and prevention program and to develop a compatible response process. The team should establish a protocol for response to critical incidents that defines the documentation and communication process.

While the team should meet on a regular basis, once the initial development process is completed, these meetings do not necessarily have to be that frequent. And not all team members need to be actively involved in every incident. A coordinator, or team leader, may have the option and the responsibility to enlist the help of particular team members as required. Regardless, there does need to be a designated process, to ensure that all members are aware of reported incidents and subsequent decisions, and have the chance to provide input.

Initiating the Threat Response Process

Few companies are organized in such a way that they naturally have the resources and skills to respond to these relatively low-frequency but high-risk events. Without a response team and a response plan in place, the organization can be quickly overwhelmed. Without an organized and deliberate approach, rushed, panic-driven decisions can be made that may actually increase and complicate the risks.

This process usually occurs under a great deal of pressure to respond quickly. There are generally some very real limitations, in terms of available time and resources. Good decision-making involving critical issues of safety have to be balanced with the need to come to decisions relatively quickly, and often with limited data. A trained response team, operating with an understanding of the appropriate protocol, and with access to the required resources, is better able to keep these concerns in balance and manage the situation safely.

It is not the purpose of this volume to train the threat response team or to offer a detailed review of the threat assessment and management process. While this book is offered as a general guide to organizations, it cannot also serve as a menu for the threat response process. There is no substitute for having a workplace violence program in place that includes a trained team, with access to available specialists. Each and every situation offers a different and generally unique framework of factors that need to be understood before they can be adequately managed. What I will present is an outline of the process as it generally occurs, but the reader should keep in mind that this is a *fluid* process that has to adapt and respond to the dynamics of the given situation.

A guiding principle throughout this process is to *not over-respond and create a greater risk*. While decisions may have to be made quickly, careful planning is critical. Time spent gathering information, in order to formulate a safe plan of approach, is generally time well spent. It will be always important to proceed carefully and in a stepwise manner. Any response or decision to intervene in any manner, even if just to interview particular individuals, should be carefully considered in light of any potential consequences that could serve to increase the risk to a member of the organization. Any response or decision should err on the side of caution and represent the least intrusive or disruptive option.

The initial review: gathering the facts

Once a report of a threat is received by the team or the team leader, the first order of business generally involves collecting information, in order to confirm and obtain the relevant details of the allegations. The initial reports have often already been skewed or distorted, and have not been subjected to any kind of confirmation process.

It is critical that decisions are based on accurate data. Effective threat management relies on an *accurate assessment*, and accurate assessment is dependent on *accurate information.* Operating on bad information will sabotage the most carefully prepared plans and can serve to catch us off guard with a suddenly unanticipated set of consequences.

Initially, the team leader, or the team member who is coordinating the particular case, is responsible for obtaining any available information, in order to make some of these initial decisions. This process would typically involve interviewing the individual who made the report, and confirming details with the appropriate managers, human resource personnel, or any others in positions of responsibility who have direct knowledge of the situation.

The initial action plan

A primary goal of any initial fact-finding review is to gather enough information to determine if there is anyone in *imminent* danger, such that emergency measures are required, like calling 911 or involving local law enforcement. Sometimes, the emotional intensity has risen to a level such that a response is immediately required that cannot wait for a more thorough review process, in order to control the risks. Employees may have to be separated or be placed on leave, pending further investigation. Regardless, there should be an understanding of the whereabouts and the current status of the subject of concern from the very beginning of this process.

At this stage following an initial review, the initial responder may determine the opposite—that the risks are negligible, such that it can be resolved on an administrative or disciplinary level, or even by no response at all. This decision should, however, still be documented and reviewed by the rest of the company's Threat Response Team.

Somewhere between these two extremes will fall most incidents, such that the data suggests a possibility of a risk that is not clearly defined and requires further investigation and more active management.

The risk assessment/management process

After the responder has accumulated available information to confirm the report and has determined that there is sufficient information to suggest that this reported event might represent a potential risk, then the risk assessment process should proceed with the critical personnel involved.

Core members of the team should be involved, including corporate security, if not already involved—as every decision from this point on affects issues of safety. If the company does not have an internal department that can address security issues, it might be wise to consider outside consultation. The company's legal counsel should be consulted throughout the process to address all the issues that can and do arise. These would preferably be attorneys who are familiar with employment law and have experience with the relative risks involved in the workplace violence response process.

The reader will note that I have not separated the assessment and the management process in the above heading. One would normally assume that the former precedes the latter, especially since we do not want to respond prematurely without adequate information and planning. However, risk assessment cannot easily be divorced from risk management in this model. The responders, for example, cannot simply go about the task of information gathering without simultaneously making decisions regarding how to keep the risks contained during this process. *Risk management occurs practically from the very beginning of the assessment process.* In fact, by the time we have completed the assessment, we have often reduced the risk considerably, such that final management decisions will sometimes be perceived as relatively anticlimactic.

After an initial accumulation of data and an understanding of the facts of the case is presented, the team should develop an internal consensus of their level of concern. It is at this point that the team may want to engage the services of a threat assessment specialist to review the available information and advise the process, based on this preliminary assessment.

At this juncture, discussions generally center around 1) how to obtain additional, needed information to complete (or at least improve) the assessment, and 2) how to successfully manage the risks during this process. Every decision regarding these issues should be developed carefully, with the goals and possible consequences (and the response to those consequences) carefully considered. The team must remain "ahead of the curve," such that they are prepared to respond to any anticipated reactions or consequences at each turn of events, with safety as the overriding concern.

Gathering information

We have previously discussed the wide range of data that must be considered as part of the threat assessment process, that must include information not only about the incident and its historical context, but also information about the individuals involved, the relevant stressors, and the contexts within which the events are occurring. During a critical event that is unfolding under a great deal of urgency, our ability to collect information is limited because of time restraints, logistics, and other issues generally related to safety concerns.

Any and all information may offer clues that can provide us with a greater understanding of the critical dynamics that may be involved. The threat assessment process has to build a picture that governs the subsequent process, and it must be based on accurate data. This assessment process often proceeds at a rapid pace and requires any and all information that is discoverable.

As can be assumed from previous chapters, the range of relevant information is practically unlimited. This assessment, while operating on relatively limited sources of information, can utilize any and all information related to the subject's background, relationship history, employment history, use and ownership of weapons, medical history, family involvement, current resources, and so on. Appendix C lists the relevant areas of concern that are generally on most threat assessment consultants' checklists.

Information will generally come from three sources: *1) people, 2) internal records, or 3) publicly available information.*

People who can provide information may include the victim (the individual threatened), witnesses, collateral contacts (which can include, but are not limited to anyone from coworkers to supervisors to family members to medical providers), or the individual of concern. From the very beginning, any interview should be carefully considered in light of its consequences: its *potential benefit* to the assessment or management process, relative to the *potential costs*. Sometimes the risks may outweigh the rewards. The closer the interviewee is personally to the subject, the greater the potential benefit, but often at a greater risk. For example, if the team decides to interview coworkers, they may gain more credible and detailed information but at a cost if the coworker cannot reliably maintain confidentiality. Even worse, the coworker's motivation may be influenced by dynamics of his or her particular relationship with the subject, the details of which may lie outside our awareness. Needless to say, interviewing family members can represent a significant risk, but offer great value in some cases.

As this investigation process proceeds, the team will be accumulating information that provides the team with a greater sense of the problem within the broader context. This generally involves interviewing the informant and carefully selected individuals. In interviews with company personnel, confidentiality is critical, and all employees interviewed should be requested to not divulge any information regarding the content of the interviews or the concerns of the investigation.

The team needs to understand the vulnerability of the

informant in each case, and how to implement a plan that does not put this informant at greater risk. Sometimes this presents a very difficult issue. Often, the source or even the nature of the information received has to be safeguarded, until the team can be assured that divulging this information does not place anyone at additional risk of retaliation.

Many informants may wish that their information be kept confidential, which cannot always be reasonably guaranteed, given the dynamics and needs of the process. In those cases, the investigators should be honest with informants and involve them in a communication loop that will keep them informed and address their concerns accordingly. The informant must be able to trust the process, and the team should therefore be responsive and attentive to this individual's concerns. Needless to say, if anyone who reports a threat believes that his or her safety was disregarded during the process, then the entire program will lose credibility in the eyes of the employees.

In gathering information from sources within the workplace, it goes without saying that the interviewer has to be continually cognizant that there are pre-existing agendas in any social setting, such that any allegation should be carefully considered. We have been involved with multiple situations in which allegations could not be confirmed, were a product of outright deception, or at the least, appeared to be heavily embellished. Understanding the interpersonal dynamics of the worksite and the motivations of those who report these threats may become a critical part of the assessment process. It is often equally important for the investigator to understand the role and involvement of the victim, in order to accurately assess the level of risk.

This first step typically involves an interview with the individual who is reporting the event, and those in responsible positions (generally managers and HR personnel) who can provide the information for the purposes of our initial needs. As the team later continues its assessment, it may decide that it needs to interview others in order to obtain the specific information for the required decisions. This should be accomplished as noted above in a careful and considered manner. This becomes more critical as we get closer to the subject, such as when interviewing collateral contacts outside the workplace who may have critical information. This should all be part of a strategic, well-considered assessment process.

Approaching the subject himself generally occurs later, unless the situation is so explosive that an intervention is recommended for reasons of safety. Interviewing the subject is a particularly critical decision that should be well-planned. The success of that interview, as will be later discussed, is dependent to some degree to the extent that the interviewer is informed and prepared.

Internal records include anything that is in the employee's file (if this is indeed an employee). Hopefully, these files have been well maintained and updated. Regardless, all of the information presented there needs to be examined with an eye to any previously overlooked data. There are often a number of pieces of information buried in the employee's original application form that can address questions that may arise through the investigative process—clues about the subject's family (who is the emergency notification?), employment history and such. Eventually, the team may even decide to contact past references again if there are concerns, as part of the process of reconstructing the subject's history. Other records include any documentation of disciplinary action, attendance issues, performance evaluations, evidence of legal actions (such as garnishments), or even health benefits records that may be legally accessible.

Publicly available records require more time and a more extensive search. This generally always occurs after the initial review, but is an essential part of any assessment process when there is a significant risk. Everyone in this field can cite many instances when those within the organization are surprised and shocked by the information received in this process, which became critical to the understanding of the subject and therefore to the decision-making process, but which was not anticipated based on any prior assumptions. Reviewed records may include, but are not limited to, civil and criminal court records (local and federal), military history, Department of Motor Vehicles records, county clerk's records, and basic Internet searches. It is important to review any information available through this process carefully. For example, it is often insufficient just to read the thumbnail descriptions or the final disposition of a legal case. Reading the complete records and transcripts of any available information can help further the investigator's understanding of the subject, and nature of the risks, if any.

The Subject Interview

In most of our cases, interviewing the subject of concern is a critical and a relatively early part of the assessment/management process, once we have obtained sufficient information to develop an approach and address relevant security issues. This is a decision that needs to be approached carefully, with adequate preparation.

Utilizing the services of a specialist who has experience and training in both threat assessment and crisis management is always preferable. In the model that we utilize, this professional should not only have strong evaluative skills, but should also be skilled and experienced in the area of crisis negotiation. During this initial contact, part of the specialist's task will be not only to assess the risk, but also hopefully to reduce it. As more is understood about what is driving this process toward a potentially violent conclusion, an experienced professional can find ways to "defuse" the individual enough to help maintain these risks at a contained or reduced level.

At this point, the threat assessment specialist can gather enough information to ascertain the general level of risk and determine the critical factors that can further guide the response planning process. Sometimes this process occurs over several contacts, as the company decides on incremental response decisions. Some consultants, myself included, are able to conduct critical initial interviews by telephone in certain well-planned circumstances. This should only occur if critical factors related to safety are well understood and addressed, the interviewer is adequately prepared, the goals are well understood, and the benefits of the contact outweigh the potential risks.

In some cases, someone who is perceived as relatively external to the immediate arena can become a less threatening point of contact for the subject. He or she can serve as a liaison of sorts and can offer to obtain information for the subject that may address his or her concerns. Having someone from outside the organization often reassures disgruntled employees that they are being heard by someone whom they perceive to be a less biased source, and further, that the company thought enough of their concerns to bring in a specialist. With more egocentric and grandiose individuals, this will sometimes serve to feed their sense of importance, which in and of itself may reduce the threat. If the subject has someone with whom he or she can discuss concerns and believes that his or her situation is being reviewed in a fair manner, then that allows a "cooling off period," that most importantly buys more time for the company's decision-making process.

Another advantage of having someone external to the organization interacting with the subject employee is that this contact may be able to identify and utilize other external resources that can provide other information—a role that the company cannot and probably should not fulfill. For example, if the subject reveals that he is under the care of a psychiatrist, the external agent may request permission to contact the psychiatrist, in order to alert this professional to the company's concerns. There are times when contacting other support systems, even including family, may benefit both the assessment and management process. Knowledge of these existing resources may prove valuable when developing response plans.

In most of our cases, the subject is placed on administrative leave during the course of this review process, with very clear requirements that he or she is not to set foot on the premises of the workplace or contact any employees, except those designated. This is critical, so that communication can be controlled and monitored. We generally prefer that this be introduced during the initial contact, as the subject's reaction may have to be managed and since his or her initial reaction may offer the interviewer valuable insight. This is a critical condition of the subject's leave agreement. If there are indications that the subject cannot reliably abide by these conditions, then this informs us a great deal about the individual and the need for security.

Often, the company may want to designate the threat assessment professional as the subject's primary (or only) contact, even if the person is external to the company. This serves to allow the specialist access to the employee, to further monitor, assess, and defuse as necessary. It also prevents any interaction with company personnel that could include potentially inflammatory discussions. Also, it places a further barrier between this individual and the company, which will allow for an easier separation process, if that represents the eventual outcome.

It is critical that the threat assessment professional represents him- or herself honestly, and adequately informs the subject as to the nature of the relationship. This consultant must not in any way imply that he or she is anything but an agent of the company. Further, the subject needs to be reminded that the discussion is not in any way confidential, and that this interaction does not represent a psychological evaluation or part of any kind of counseling process. Further, the subject should understand that this is a voluntary interview that has been requested by his or her employer.

Remaining honest with the subject of concern has far more benefits than simply ethical or legal ones. Cooperation and eventual resolution works when a respectful relationship is established, that requires a degree of trust in the process. The best way to interact with suspicious or even paranoid people is to be as open and honest as possible. If an alienated and distrustful subject receives evidence verifying that he or she is being deceived, then any opportunity to maintain that relationship, and to therefore effectively assess and manage the situation, is essentially lost. This is not to imply that we have to reveal all known information, but deception should be rigorously avoided.

Response Strategies

Strategizing the company's response occurs from the very beginning, as the responders begin determining how to collect more information and control the risks. As noted above, the response team, or the primary responder, may decide on an emergency 911 action, or may even decide to forgo any kind of subsequent intervention. While generally a subject interview is a preferred and early intervention in our model, this interview may become unnecessary or even discouraged for a number of reasons, including safety. Again, this is not a standardized process. It must remain fluid enough to respond to the situation, which underscores the involvement of a trained team under professional and experienced advisement.

In our model, the initial intervention most often involves an interview with the subject as noted above, usually by someone trained in threat assessment. During that interview, the interviewer is able to gather the information adequate to advise the subsequent process. More often than not, the interviewer may be able to stabilize the individual enough to provide the team more time to put together a plan.

A frequently asked question is: When should the company call in a specialist? At what point does the risk rise to a level, such that an external threat assessment professional is contacted? There is no easy answer to that question, for it will depend on the skills and experience of the company's response team. Some organizations have very well-trained and experienced teams that have worked on multiple cases and have a good sense of both their skills and their limitations. Due to this experience, they often have a close working relationship with a threat assessment professional, someone who has helped train the team, to the point that this specialist can sometimes simply serve as a remote advisor. Other organizations do not have this kind of experience or may prefer to rely heavily on outside consultation.

Response plans can range from doing nothing at all (i.e. "wait and see"), in which a monitoring system is established, to a highly confrontational intervention involving law enforcement.

In between these extremes, where most cases lie, are *innumerable* possibilities, depending on the specific dynamics of the situation. The selected plan relies on the guidance of the assessment process.

The company may decide to seek legal remedies, such as protective or restraining orders. It may decide to have the subject undergo more extensive medical or psychological evaluations, mandate medical treatment or even consider initiating an involuntary commitment process. It may decide to enlist the help of outside agencies, or even the subject's family. It may decide to simply rely on the organization's existing disciplinary process, or it may decide to negotiate a voluntary separation process. The company may have to make decisions regarding the protection of potential victims, including relocation, or initiate a surveillance process. It will certainly have to continually address the security needs of the company's employees or even those outside the organization throughout this process, and respond appropriately. These actions represent just a very few examples of the range of possible actions that can occur, that are always dependent on the assessment process and the needs of the particular situation.

Through the course of his or her assessment, the threat assessment professional will not just have a better understanding of the level and nature of the risks involved. Ideally, this assessment process will further elucidate the particular *needs* of the individual and the relevant characteristics of his or her particular situation, which will be of benefit throughout this process. What can often occur is something that is akin to a negotiation process, or at least utilizes the primary elements of that process. As the subject's needs are better identified, a resolution can be formulated that can help reduce the subject's anger and facilitate a more cooperative response—and therefore a safer outcome.

The timing of any action by the threat response team in these emotionally laden situations is critical. The eventual success of any intervention is facilitated by the subject's cooperation, and if the subject has been prepared to a certain extent. As any specialist in crisis negotiation or dispute resolution knows, the subject's cooperation is dependent often on a preparatory interactive process. Ideally, we would like for this individual to be at a "place" where he or she has some understanding of the rationale for these actions and is not too destabilized by these actions, even if the subject does not agree with them. We have therefore found that having a specialist engage with the subject early in the process in order to monitor, assess, inform, and defuse this individual helps to assure that the process occurs smoothly and on the right timetable.

We are always eventually interested in long-term solutions if at all possible, not just a short-term Band-Aid. This is particularly true when an employee is being separated and the company wants to be assured that its other employees are not exposed to any long-term danger. Whenever possible, we want to achieve as close to a "win-win" as possible, borrowing a term from dispute resolution literature. We want to eventually ensure that all involved parties can walk away without having to look over their shoulders. This will be discussed in more detail in the chapter on terminations.

At this investigative stage, the company wants to take a relatively "soft" approach with the subject, while taking a "hard" approach in terms of the rules and expected behaviors during the investigation process. The subject is constantly assured that the company wants to conduct a fair and respectful investigation and to be respectful of the rights of that particular individual. A paid, as opposed to an unpaid, leave (as opposed to suspension) is usually preferred. The person who reaches out to the subject needs to have the skills in order to present a positive, supportive approach and to be careful not to inflame or otherwise increase the risk. In return, the subject must understand that certain rules will be strictly enforced during this review process in order to maintain safety. Again, borrowing a phrase from the dispute resolution literature, we want to be "soft on the people and hard on the problems."

This process proceeds as noted, in a stepwise manner. As decisions are developed and new information is obtained, the team continually regroups. Strategies change, as this is a dynamic situation in which more information is being obtained and in which the process itself affects the critical variables. Information gathering, and the assessment process in general, continues generally throughout.

Return-to-Work Decisions

Once the incident has been safely managed, decisions will have to be made regarding how, when, and if the employee is to return to work. In these situations, this only occurs when the assessment is completed and any residual issues regarding risks are addressed to everyone's satisfaction. Any return should be carefully planned, with the needs of all the employees considered. The transition back to work may present some problems in terms of existing relationships, and in light of what may have occurred, even if there are no further risks.

When and if the employee is brought back to work, it is highly recommended that the company and the employee arrive at a contractual understanding. The company's expectations regarding the employee's future behavior, along with the consequences of any infractions, should be spelled out clearly and completely. This agreement would include any future obligations that have been identified in the assessment process as critical to the prevention of further problems. The possible conditions listed in this agreement are numerous and depend on the nature of the identified risk and the relevant contributory factors. This may include, but is not limited to, mandated review meetings with human resources, drug screens, counseling, and a variety of other options that can serve to monitor the employee and prevent future problems.

We recommend very highly that the terms of this agreement be put in writing and require the employee's signature. One example of a Return-to-Work Agreement is presented in Appendix D.

It may be clear at some point that it is in everyone's best interests to voluntarily separate. In many cases, the employee may decide that returning to work is not preferable, and would like to have the opportunity to resign. Many employees in these circumstances have a long history of performance or relationship problems with the company, but may have had difficulty moving on, due to financial, psychological, or other concerns. The company may decide to come to an agreement with such an employee, if it appears that this separation represents something of mutual value. Again, understanding the employee's needs will be useful when crafting a solution that helps the employee exit with his or her self-esteem intact. Helping the employee in the transition can be mutually beneficial (and cost-effective) in many of these situations. This *process itself* will help to ensure that the employee leaves with the belief that the organization treated him or her in a considerate and fair manner.

I always recommend contractual agreements when separating with employees under these kinds of circumstances, whether voluntary or not. Agreements with terminated employees will be discussed in more detail in the next chapter, but the relevant issues are generally applicable to resignations also. There is always, at the very least, a benefit in clarifying the respective parties' expectations, along with any conditions or contingencies, especially when finalizing a relationship. And it is recommended that this indeed represent a "final" interaction, as a complete separation is always preferred. Ideally, the company wants to adequately address all pertinent issues to everyone's satisfaction, in order to close that door without second thoughts or concerns about future risks. Separation agreements, as represented in Appendix E, will be discussed in the upcoming chapter on terminations.

If the company decides that it has grounds for termination, or if an arrangement is made with the employee to separate in some manner, then it is generally recommended that the employee not physically return to the company for any reason. Once a physical separation has occurred, as part of this threat management process, the employee has likely already been engaging in an emotional separation process which should not be disrupted. This will be discussed in detail in the following chapter on safe terminations.

Monitoring and Follow-up

At all times throughout the assessment process, the team needs to remain cognizant of the level of risk that the situation presents at that particular point in time. As noted in Chapter 2, these are fluid situations in which assessment is always based on situational factors that can change. Having someone who is interacting with and monitoring this individual is critical if the investigation process is prolonged, in order to address any issues that threaten to destabilize the situation.

The response team should be aware that if an employee is out on leave for an extended period under a cloud of uncertainty, without any understanding of the process, it can have a critical effect on his or her emotional stability. No one should remain out on leave without periodic contact with a designated party, especially if their access to the company has been restricted.

Post-intervention monitoring is when denial can again become operational. Once the immediate danger passes and our attention becomes diverted to other issues, it is relatively easy to operate under an unspoken and dangerous assumption that the problem has been resolved. Monitoring the outcome of interventions and managing the subsequent consequences is most critical, but is an easily neglected part of the process. All too often, there is an assumption that no news is good news. Almost every intervention, whether active or passive, requires adequate follow-up and a planned monitoring process.

If an employee has returned to work under a Return-to-Work Agreement, there must exist a follow-up process to ensure that the situation remains safe and that the requirements of the response plan are being met. If an individual who has been identified as high-risk and with limited resources has been separated from the company, long-term safety coverage requires some kind of subsequent monitoring plan, which will also be addressed in the chapter on terminations.

Debriefing and process review

When the critical incident is in the final stages of resolution, it is advantageous at that point for the relevant team members to review and document what has occurred and to conduct a debriefing in order to discuss the events, the solutions, what worked, and what did not work. This is a period when the most effective learning occurs. There will often be information received that suggests a breakdown in the reporting or prevention systems, which may require a review, with follow-up actions and subsequent reviews. As noted in the section on monitoring, this meeting needs to identify any subsequent and ongoing responsibilities.

The Threat Assessment Professional

There are those who specialize in the area of threat assessment and threat management, who actually assist organizations on these types of issues on a daily basis. Many are psychologists or psychiatrists with a forensic and/or clinical background, but there are others who have achieved their specialized skills through law enforcement and similar experience and training. This is not yet a clearly-defined area of professional practice, and there is little in the way of credentialing or formalized instruction. It was only recently, in 1992, that the Association of Threat Assessment Professionals was founded as an organization dedicated to enhancing the knowledge of those in this field.

The academic credentials of this specialist, while important, are often secondary to his or her experience in this particular arena. A vast majority of mental health professionals, for example, do *not* automatically have the specific skills or experience to operate in this area of specialty, even with extensive academic credentials. Further, many security and management consultants may expand their services into this area without the necessary skills, training, and experience.

Further, many of those who do specialize in this area may be limited in regard to what services that they can offer to the organization. For example, there are forensic psychologists and psychiatrists who are quite proficient in the area of evaluation and even threat assessment, but may not necessarily have experience in defusing hostile individuals or in actively managing situations involving conflict. There are those who may have an extensive background in crisis management or even hostage negotiation, but who do not have experience in consulting with organizations or in managing the nature of events that are more likely to occur within the workplace.

Finally, in order to adequately address the varied demands that these incidents may present, these professionals often have to have a range of rather diverse skills and experience, the combination of which is relatively rare in the professional community. Based on the model that we utilize, this professional must be able to shift easily from threat assessor to crisis negotiator to case manager to organizational consultant, depending on the demands of the situation.

There are many benefits to utilizing the services of an external professional who specializes in threat assessment and management:

- *Threat Assessment.* Determining whether someone represents an actual threat is a difficult and rather specialized evaluative skill. It is not typically a part of most psychological or psychiatric evaluations, and involves consideration of a wider range of data.
- *Formulating Response Strategy.* Based on their assessment, this professional can help advise management as to the most effective response to reduce risks to the company and its employees.
- *Defusing Anger.* As part of, and subsequent to, the assessment process, the consultant can engage the subject to help manage and reduce the threat. In many situations involving conflict, a third party can usually de-escalate and negotiate with angry individuals in a more effective and expeditious manner than is possible (or desirable) by those within the organization.

- *Monitoring.* An external consultant will be better able to monitor and follow up with a potentially violent employee by having a less restricted access to outside resources and to the subject himself. This is particularly critical with those who are not employed or are no longer employed by the company.
- *Disengagement.* Many incidents involving terminated employees are complicated because the individual cannot effectively separate from the company. The company is therefore not able to aid in that separation without a risk of reinforcing the relationship or even inflaming the subject.
- *Coordination of resources.* An outside consultant can manage and coordinate external resources in a way that management cannot or perhaps should not. In the case of separated employees, it is generally not to the company's advantage to engage in any manner that encourages a continued relationship.

The ADA and Other Legal Concerns

As various legal issues can and do arise during this process, consultation with the company's legal counsel is critical to the success of this kind of high-risk intervention, which can involve a variety of different risks at every turn. This legal representative should be consulted early, as opposed to later, in this process. It can be quite frustrating whenever anyone is brought in for an opinion at a late date and is charged with the duty of reviewing and potentially reversing plans painstakingly developed over a significant period, but with a flawed understanding of relevant legal issues. This also provides the company's legal consultant experience in the nuances of the threat response process, if they do not already have that experience.

Involvement of legal counsel early in the decision-making process also facilitates their understanding of the safety issues that are at stake in this particular incident. They will therefore become more acutely aware of the relative and often conflicting issues of risk management that can often occur in these situations. There are certainly events in which safety issues may conflict with legal concerns, in which the team decides that it is "better to be tried by twelve (a jury) than carried by six (pallbearers)" (Corcoran & Cawood, 2003).

There are sometimes concerns about the Americans with Disabilities Act (ADA), in relation to our assessment and intervention process. The questions that are generally raised concern the issue of whether we are somehow legally exposing the company by the nature of our investigation process (i.e., involving a psychologist or psychiatrist), or by even addressing these behaviors. Are we are risking a claim that these behaviors are somehow related to a medically determinable mental condition, and therefore subject to some kind of accommodation?

In regards to the ADA issue, I have included an opinion in the box below, which is offered by Chad Shultz, a labor and employment law attorney, who specializes in this specific area of concern.

First and foremost, it remains always critical that we concentrate on specific *work-related behaviors* that represent a *safety risk* to the workplace. It is *not* the threat assessment professional's position to diagnose or otherwise attribute behaviors to any kind of mental or physical condition, regardless of his or her area of professional expertise.

If the employee wants to somehow allege that his or her behaviors are related to a medical condition that requires accommodation, then certainly the employee is encouraged to seek legal, medical, or psychological consultation regarding that issue; however, our primary issue is always the issue of *safety* and the impact of the subject's behavior on that primary issue. I personally have never in all of my experience consulted on a case that resulted in an ADA claim. If the case is managed in an appropriate manner, the issue of ADA should not generally represent a predominant concern.

Sometimes, an individual is referred for what is termed a psychological "Fitness for Duty" evaluation as part of the company's response to behaviors exhibited by that employee. This represents a particular medical/psychological evaluation whose purpose is to identify any psychological factors that may impede that individual's ability to perform the essential elements of his or her job effectively. This is a comprehensive diagnostic evaluation; it addresses any mental health or medical condition that may be interfering with the employee's ability to carry out all the essential duties of his or her position. This evaluation can be recommended as part of the response plan if the situation warrants it, but it is *not* necessarily part and parcel of a threat assessment process. For a more thorough review of Fitness for Duty evaluations, refer to the excellent text on this subject by Anthony Stone (2000). (See Bibliography for details.)

An opinion by the EEOC is very clear on this subject: *"[An employer may discipline an individual with a disability] provided that the workplace conduct standard is job-related for the position in question and is consistent with business necessity. For example, nothing in the ADA prevents an employer from maintaining a workplace free of violence or threats of violence..."* In a specific example, this opinion concluded that the employer could terminate the employee for bringing a loaded gun onto company property, *"assuming it would impose such discipline on employees without disabilities."* It further makes clear that *"traits or behaviors are not, in themselves, mental impairments."*[1]

Workplace Violence and the ADA

There is often an assumption that the Americans with Disabilities Act of 1990 (ADA) somehow limits the ability of employers to control workplace violence. In actuality, the ADA has very little, if any, impact on the issue of workplace violence.

The ADA was promulgated to protect "qualified" individuals with a disability from discrimination based on such disability (42 U.S.C. §§ 12101-12213). To be "qualified" the individual must be able to perform the essential functions

---

of the job with or without a reasonable accommodation (42 U.S.C. § 12111(8)). In addition, the employee must not pose a direct threat to the health or safety of himself or others (*Chevron U.S.A., Inc. v. Echazaba*, 536 U.S. 73, 2002). Employees who act violently or threaten violence pose a direct threat and cannot be reasonably accommodated *(see Sullivan v. River Valley School District*, 197 F.3d 804, 813, 6th Cir., 1999; *Palmer v. Circuit Court of Cook County*, 117 F.3d 351, 352, 7th Cir., 1997).

The ADA does not, therefore, require an employer to retain violent or potentially violent employees (*Palmer v. Circuit Court of Cook County*, 117 F.3d 351, 352, 7th Cir., 1997). These employees are not "qualified" for the job, even if they have a disability. To find otherwise would place employers in the impossible position of choosing between firing the employee and violating the ADA or retaining the employee and being found negligent (*Id.* 352).

Chad Shultz
Ford & Harrison, LLC

A final word about legal issues

These are typically highly emotional situations, often with a history of conflict and accusations, which can threaten to become litigious at multiple points. This is certainly, next to safety issues, a primary source of apprehension for every employer. However, while threats of lawsuits may be hurled during the initial stages of these events, this has generally not been the end result. In actuality, we often encourage and welcome a decision to seek representation, especially by an individual who has been identified as being at high risk for violent behavior. In most cases, it places the individual in a process that should help control the risks—and it certainly compares favorably to the alternative.

I believe that we have not experienced lawsuits for two

primary reasons. One, we believe that it is important that the company proceeds in a legally defensible manner at every step of the process. A careful approach by a trained team under professional advisement helps to ensure that. Secondly, in every intervention in which we are involved, we strive to achieve the feeling of a *"win-win,"* in which the affected parties believe that they were treated *fairly and respectfully.*

Even in the most contentious, long-term cases, the goal is to go beyond just preventing any immediate danger, and to work toward what would be considered a *resolution.* We always attempt to identify the fundamental needs of those involved, even (and especially) the subject who is at risk. We eventually attempt to look beyond the demands and the loud allegations of the present event, in order to determine what response might also address this individual's underlying and fundamental interests. These individuals eventually have to move on with their lives, and we want them to do so in a manner that does not create or enhance a future risk of harm to anyone. This is the best approach, and it works to *everyone's* benefit!

Endnotes

[1] From EEOC Notice Number 915.002, March 25, 1997, ADA Division, Office of Legal Counsel.

Chapter 6

Safe Terminations

The Crisis of Job Loss

Terminating someone's employment and having to bear witness to the resulting emotional aftermath is never an easy task for any manager. The loss of a job carries with it a serious, potentially frightening avalanche of other losses, all of which can be further compounded by other critical factors such as availability of other employment, the economy, the age of the employee, the needs of his or her dependents, and so forth.

Beyond all of these considerations, a person's job means even more than all of that. Our job is generally part and parcel of our identity. It helps to define, for many of us, *who we are!* Despite idealistic views of an individual's intrinsic value, to lose one's job can disrupt our definition of our perceived value. When making a new acquaintance, we typically want to know: "And *what do you do?*" Our perception of that person will incorporate that knowledge, and influence subsequent assumptions about him or her. Needless to say, being "unemployed" or "between jobs" carries little status and is generally not socially valued. It can be a scary experience, especially for those with dependents.

This is all in addition to the fact that the job is where many of us spend a large portion, if not most, of our waking hours, and where we often develop a community of relationships. This loss is particularly significant if the separated employee is experiencing the effects of other losses or is simply without other critical resources and support structures in his or her life. Individuals may find themselves suddenly back at home, overwhelmed and with a profound and real sense of loss—with literally nothing to do and nowhere to go.

No amount of severance or monetary consideration can compensate for the feelings of inadequacy that adults feel when they are suddenly without a job. Even if there is some relief, and even if there is a separation package, the need for meaningful activity is secondary only to the need for survival—and the loss of work may threaten both. At some point down the road, even those who appear to accept the termination with relatively little reaction may ultimately experience feelings of resentment, when their self-worth and emotional stability become threatened by an extended period of unemployment.

The price of loyalty

Not only do we identify with our profession, we may also identify with our particular job and with our particular employer. Organizations often ask for loyalty from their employees and encourage an identification with the company and with other employees within the company. As noted in Chapter 2, we often find that having employees who are *overly attached* to the organization carries a higher level of risk if these employees are suddenly separated from the job that provides them with their sense of worth and governs a huge portion of their identity.

We have found that in some communities, employees of certain companies wear their work uniforms off-hours, with the insignias displayed with pride, as a sign of their success. Others have decorated their homes with company-specific memorabilia, which may constitute their only "hobby."

This job loss can be particularly notable when the company enjoys a relatively high-status position within the community, when the employee loses a job that may have represented the "pinnacle" of his or her success. These separated employees may come to a realization (which may be accurate) that they are not likely to find a position that is as rewarding as what they have enjoyed in the past, financially or in terms of their perceived status. The loss is doubled in that they are not only subjected to the shame of being terminated, but their new position represents a demotion of sorts.

Many grow to rely on their relationships within the company as their *primary* relationships, and may refer to the organization as their "family." This identification certainly may have served to benefit the company during their period of employment, but a price for this loyalty is paid at termination. Separating these employees takes on the emotional crisis of any major, unwanted family separation—one of several reasons that interest in the employee's support system is often a critical part of the threat assessment process during these events.

Separating High-Risk Employees

All of the above being said, there are certain employees who raise special concerns, beyond the ordinary—concerns that this employee will react in an inappropriate, rage-filled, or retaliatory manner. This is particularly the case when abusive or bullying employees are finally confronted and terminated. The end result is the apprehension that everyone has always experienced around this individual—the fear that has been at the root of the company's prior avoidance of any kind of adverse action.

Sometimes our concerns are difficult to define and may even be dismissed as just a "gut feeling," subsequently convincing ourselves that we are "overreacting" with no clear evidence to support a legitimate concern. Sometimes, the company terminates employees in which the concerns are not so much about their immediate emotional reaction, as there are concerns about a more fundamental social or character disturbance—that this individual may have the means, personality, and motivation to strategically plan and carry out an act of revenge.

There are a variety of scenarios that can be assumed under the heading of a "high-risk" termination, which can give a manager pause. It is imperative that the management do just that: *pause ...* before proceeding into a potentially inflammatory process.

Proceeding with caution

We have already discussed the common error of denying or avoiding problems that we do not wish to confront, and many terminations may be long overdue for that reason. However, even with these employees, the organization must be on guard against the *second most common error* (after denial and avoidance): the error of *acting too hastily,* in an effort to make the problem quickly "go away." Separating an employee identified as potentially at risk without a careful review invites a potential cavalcade of disastrous events that one cannot undo.

The separation process is usually the employer's last chance to effectively interact with this particular individual, and further, to adequately assess and understand some of the important issues that are involved, particularly ones that are related to the potential for violence. It is also the last opportunity to influence the situation in a preventative or proactive manner.

Once the termination occurs, the company no longer has a relationship with this employee and certainly has little in the way of leverage. The just-separated ex-employee is hardly one who is motivated to engage in a dialogue, and will reject any attempt at a relationship, other than one that springs from his or her immediate, more reactive needs. The person will be defensive and hurt, and may be emotionally destabilized—certainly not inclined to become engaged in a cooperative problem-solving process with the organization. Further, the organization would be ill-advised to engage in any process that continues to reinforce a relationship, for obvious reasons.

Engaging with an ex-employee in order to assess or somehow accomplish an intervention is always problematic. Many times, the damage is done and the employee is hurt, angry, and hardly inclined to communicate with the employer or its consultants, as there exist no recognizable incentives to do so. In more urgent scenarios, we may have a situation that is rapidly destabilizing, with no safeguards or contingency plans in place.

Pause... Assess... Confer... Plan

The first rule of thumb in any termination is to take a breath and not rush into it. Before we begin the separation process with a potentially high-risk employee, we have to make certain that we have completed an assessment that addresses our concerns to the greatest degree possible, and to our satisfaction. If we decide to wait until after the termination, we have relatively few options or leverage to assess or influence or monitor a situation that may quickly destabilize.

The value of simply taking a pause and conferencing with others cannot be overstated. This, once again, appears to run contrary to a rather typical, almost instinctual response that many of us have witnessed: the desire to drive this to a quick conclusion. It appears to be motivated by a desire to simply rid ourselves of this disagreeable, potentially dangerous person, as if sending him or her packing will truly end the problem.

If the employer has concerns about a particular employee, the first step would be to assemble whatever information is available, and to conference with those personnel who are responsible for making decisions in high-risk situations. A manager may want to first confer with a peer, to help verbalize, clarify, and confirm any concerns. Through this communication process, management will arrive at a clearer idea of some of the critical issues, both internal and external to the organization, which may not be initially apparent.

It is often remarkable how well the denial process works. When first consulted regarding a particular case, there is often an initial apology of sorts, with the company's representative alluding to a relatively minor problem that is "probably no big deal." However, once the manager begins presenting the evidence (which generally is of greater quantity than anyone in the room initially realized), there is suddenly a recognition that was not there before—that this is indeed a situation that *could be dangerous.* From the beginning, there existed a preponderance of evidence that was not fully appreciated in its entirety until it was verbalized, recorded, or otherwise shared with others.

If there exist continuing concerns that this individual may represent a significant risk, it would be most appropriate to consult the company's threat management team or at least to review these concerns with human resources, management, and legal. It is during these times that a team approach is most critical. Termination must be planned carefully, in conference with all critical personnel to *ensure* that the process will proceed safely. Each step of the separation process should be carefully considered, in regard to any possible consequences or points in the process that could serve to destabilize it.

This is not the time to shortcut the risk assessment process. If an employee is considered at risk and is facing the most adverse employment action possible, and will soon be released into the community without any way to monitor his or her intentions or whereabouts, the threat management team needs to consider professional consultation.

Once the assessment is completed and the termination is planned, it needs to be rehearsed, and everyone in the planning process should be satisfied that they have sufficiently considered all of the available evidence, have addressed the critical issues and options, and have considered and prepared for the consequences of their decisions. The decision makers should be satisfied that they have sufficiently addressed the relevant issues and feel confident that they would be able to defend their decisions in any court of law.

Separate completely

Any separation process should strive for a complete separation, in which there is no mechanism built into the termination that may act to reinforce a direct relationship with the company. If the ex-employee has to contact the organization, it should only occur through designated, previously agreed-upon channels. Those designated points of contact need to be coached as to their responses and the limits of the communications. We want these ex-employees to successfully move on, with as few opportunities as possible to revisit any past negative feelings or issues, or engage in any interaction that could possibly inflame them or otherwise undermine that separation process.

This may prove difficult for both this employee and others within the company, but it rarely serves any purpose to actively continue a relationship with an individual identified as high-risk. We all want to "bring closure," and I have known organizations that have expressed genuine concern for the separated employee. They have expressed concern that the subject needs "time to grieve" or to otherwise process this experience with the employer in general or with other employees specifically.

The recovery process that occurs subsequent to this kind of experience can be a lengthy one, in which the separated employee will advance through a series of emotional stages. Rarely is the ex-employee (or anyone in the organization) well served by sharing this experience with those who remain in the organization. There will be times of resentment and anger that may or may not be rational or justified, and cannot be satisfied or resolved by prolonging the relationship. The ex-employee needs to truly move on and exit the relationship. The employer is not in a position to effectively help this person in the recovery process in any direct capacity.

The company may decide to build into the separation agreement conditions that require interaction with the ex-employee after the termination. These are typically for specific purposes, as part of an effort to monitor and/or aid this individual in his or her transition. These interactions should generally be accomplished through agents of the company or resources that the company and its agents have arranged. Many companies prefer that the outside threat management consultant continue to serve as the primary or sometimes only contact for the employee. This consultant can then monitor and influence events without the company having to directly communicate with the individual.

Consider contractual agreements

If the company decides to terminate an employee when there are extenuating concerns (such as safety), it would always be advisable not to proceed with this action without a thorough understanding of any conditions or expectations that would be applicable, after the employee leaves. This is particularly the case in these high-risk terminations, as we want to ensure a complete separation without any misunderstandings or ambiguity that could serve to destabilize the process.

These expectations can best be delineated through a formalized agreement. This agreement should certainly be reviewed and/or prepared by the company's attorney, who will typically want to include the standard language and protections. All of the company's expectations and obligations should be clarified in this document. If the employee is expected not to physically approach the company or contact nondesignated employees (as is always recommended), this can be clearly spelled out in this agreement.

In a contentious termination process, there generally has to be some kind of incentive to motivate a separated employee to agree to any kind of terms. As we have discussed, a careful and considered assessment process can result in an understanding of specific needs of the separated employee that can possibly be addressed through this agreement. The company may decide to offer extended insurance coverage, outplacement counseling, or even some kind of severance arrangement if the company believes this to be justified. Any offers of help by the company should be conditional on a set of clear obligations that the employee has to fulfill, such as not approaching the workplace or other employees, attending stress management counseling, or any commitment that helps to ensure a safe and effective separation for everyone.

The road to this agreement is usually paved by the threat assessment process. The assessment process can be used to not only clarify the level of risk, but also to identify critical needs of the subject employee. Certainly, not all of these cases will respond to these techniques or arrive at a resolution that satisfies the ex-employee, who is after all, losing his or her job. However, the process can address critical issues that can serve to reduce the risks for the organization. Further, engaging the employee in this process will many times in itself, sufficiently de-escalate and even sufficiently satisfy some of the employee's issues.

Think long-term

Many of the more dramatic incidences of workplace violence have involved employees who have returned many months (even years) after separation. It is therefore critical to consider any significant long-range consequences of the termination that may affect our concerns about safety.

It is often insufficient to simply place some kind of "Band-Aid" on a short-term need of the employee and believe that we have protected ourselves. Simply "buying off" an employee, for example, is not a recommended action if it is not part of a carefully considered overall plan that seeks to address the long-range concerns of the company. An angry employee who is identified as at risk of seeking revenge will not automatically walk away just because he or she received some cash—especially when the cash eventually runs out!

In fact, any kind of *routine* response that does not take into account the critical variables of the presenting situation and is not part of an overall plan invites problems. For example, routinely providing severance payments to terminated dangerous employees can be a knee-jerk reaction that ignores the specific requirements of the particular situation, does not address the long-term issues, and may set a problematic precedent for the organization. It may represent an attempt by the organization to shortcut a more deliberate and careful assessment process.

As with the planning of all threat-related critical incidents, there is no default response, and it is difficult to delineate all the creative ways in which one can manage a particular situation. This is particularly true when developing contractual agreements with separated employees that are designed to address the company's long-range needs. There are ways to establish mechanisms during and after the termination process, which will help to alert us if they become unstable or retaliatory, typically through external resources. Much of this is dependent on understanding the terminated employee and his or her needs, but much of it is also facilitated by simply engaging the person in a *process* that in itself will serve to defuse and reduce the risk of retaliation.

Consider external support services

To cover the short and long-term needs of the ex-employee and the associated safety concerns of the company, consider enlisting the help of external support services that would be appropriate to the needs of the individual, such as mental health counseling, community support services, and outplacement help, as examples. There are agencies that can help the employee achieve a successful separation that does not necessitate direct interaction with the company itself, which is always counterproductive.

There are several contacts and referrals that can be particularly useful. If the ex-employee is under medical or psychological treatment, for example, his or her treatment provider is under some professional obligation to make certain that the patient does not present a risk to harm him- or herself or others, and is generally assumed to have a duty to warn potential victims. Outplacement counseling cannot be recommended strongly enough, for the simple reason that when someone finds other employment, then the threat to the former employer typically disappears.

There are sometimes concerns that by mandating or referring someone to counseling after he or she has been separated, we are somehow risking an ADA (Americans with Disabilities Act) claim. Any kind of required or recommended counseling after termination is related to either the emotional stress that may be secondary to the separation, or specific safety-related behaviors that are of concern, and not because of any diagnosed mental condition. The company's threat assessment process is not designed to diagnose or address psychological conditions; its sole aim is to assess the degree of risk and to make recommendations to reduce that risk.

Other external agencies that may be of benefit are those related to the legal system. Law enforcement and the court system may become a part of the post-termination containment planning, most evident when an employer decides to obtain a protective or restraining order. The employee may be under probation for some prior offense, such that his or her probation officer can serve as a useful point of contact. The threat of violating probation and losing one's freedom acts as an effective motivator and control. On rare occasions, the ex-employee's family may become an integral part of both the pre- or post-termination process. Certain family members may voluntarily surface during this process, who are concerned and are willing to help the employee stay out of trouble. As previously noted, enlisting the help of family members should be carefully considered.

Be fair and respectful

This appears to be simple and perhaps obvious advice, but some of these individuals have engaged in such inappropriate behavior for so long, that the most forgiving of us can barely avoid not just kicking them out the door, with one final gesture. Otherwise knowledgeable and competent managers have been known to become very emotionally reactive during the termination process, sometimes engaging in a shouting match that considerably raises the risk of retaliation.

All too often, there is an understandable reluctance to "reward" abusive employees in any way, but this attitude will come at a cost. We always have to weigh the potential risks, and if treating someone fairly and respectfully leads to increased safety, then this is a small price to pay. No matter what our feelings are about this particular employee, termination is our last chance to interact with and influence this particular individual. This final interaction will linger in the memory of the separated employee and can, over time, become the focal point of the individual's self-justification for revenge.

The chance that a separated employee will walk away and not engage in retaliatory behavior is always increased if the employee believes that he or she has been treated in a fair and respectful manner during the termination process, regardless of what may have occurred prior to the termination. We do not want any of our employees to leave work and walk into the parking lot looking over their shoulder.

A Case Example

A recent case from our files may help to illustrate one example of the results of this process, at least for this particular situation:

> Consultation was requested on a case of an employee who believed that he was about to be terminated due to longstanding performance issues (which was actually a correct assumption). He had verbalized a threat to a coworker that he would kill himself and his managers if that termination were carried out.
>
> When management received word of the threat, they decided to delay termination (which had been planned for the next day) and enlisted our services to help conduct a risk assessment. A subsequent series of interviews with this and other employees revealed a highly stressed employee who was determined to be at risk for suicide if his employment was indeed terminated. The chance that he would commit this act at work and injure or kill others in the process was considered quite possible. Further, he kept a weapon in his car, and he held a longstanding grudge against one of his supervisors for some perceived injustices that had occurred in the past. Even if he did not immediately retaliate, his emotional condition was such that it may have interfered with his ability to land other employment, thus raising concerns about the future.
>
> Based on our recommendations, the company delayed the termination and suspended the employee, in order to further investigate the alleged threat and complete the risk assessment. The company decided to continue to pay him during this suspension as long as the employee continued

to cooperate with the process, remained in communication and compliant with the company's consultant, and agreed to not approach the company or any of its employees during this process.

Due to concerns about the employee's emotional stability, he was referred to a local mental health provider. The employee went willingly and was accompanied by a coworker/friend, and agreed to release his treatment provider to discuss with the company's consultant any issues related to compliance and/or risks to the company or its employees. (If the employee had not gone voluntarily, the company had a plan to engage local law enforcement to help escort the employee to the local hospital for an evaluation, due to concerns about the possibility of suicide and/or homicide.)

The psychologist at the mental health center determined that the employee required treatment for an adjustment disorder. He was depressed due to a recent series of events in his personal and family life. His wife was diagnosed with cancer, and his child was dependent on medication due to a chronic condition. While he was threatened with the loss of the income from his job, he was even more concerned (understandably) about their continuing medical care and whether he would be able to afford other insurance coverage.

The company decided in this situation to postpone the termination, and the employee was placed on short-term disability until his condition was stabilized and his medical provider determined that he was not restricted from working due to his emotional condition. The employee, in the meantime, was engaged in a continuing dialogue with the company's threat assessment consultant, who monitored his progress, with the help of the local mental health provider. Through this process, the employee's anger was reduced considerably, and other community support services were engaged. The employee came to the conclusion that the company was treating him in a fair and generous manner, and he was further able to express and resolve some of his work-related concerns, particularly in regards to the aforementioned supervisor. The mental health provider was able to help the employee in his adjustment to his many losses, along with the probability of his upcoming job loss.

The company proceeded with the termination for the above-mentioned performance issues, once the employee had stabilized, and when he was medically released by his psychologist. By this point, he had come to a clearer understanding and acceptance of the realities of the eventual termination and was more emotionally prepared, and had more resources at his disposal.

At the recommendation of the threat assessment consultant, the company decided to offer this individual extended insurance coverage beyond what was normally offered, essentially as a gift to this employee in view of his family's extenuating health concerns. The employer also paid for a month of outplacement counseling services, to help the employee with his subsequent job search. The employer also agreed not to contest any application for unemployment benefits.

These extra benefits were offered as part of a contractual agreement, whereby the employee agreed that in order to receive these benefits, especially the extended insurance coverage, that he must continue to be engaged in psychological treatment to help him manage the stress of post-termination, for the duration of this agreement or until his therapist released him. He further agreed to continue to allow his psychologist to discuss with the company's consultant any issues relevant to his compliance and any risks to the company. The now ex-employee agreed to remain in continued contact with the company's consultant (not the company), who would monitor his compliance and overall progress. The agreement included a recognition that he was not to contact other employees or set foot on company property.

The employee believed this to be a relatively fair agreement. He continued to have difficulty accepting that his performance was such that it required termination, but he appreciated the company's flexibility and consideration, in light of the other stressors in his life, and he did not fault the company or any particular employee.

This above example represents only one of *innumerable* arrangements that can arise, in which the company carefully formulates a comprehensive plan that helps to address its long-term safety concerns. The above scenario resulted in an agreement that was mutually agreeable, at least to the extent that the ex-employee was able to exit the process believing that some fundamental concerns were addressed in a respectful manner.

As noted, we strive for a "win-win" as much as is possible in these very difficult circumstances. Granted, the employee does not get his or her job back, but is able to leave, believing that he or she was treated respectfully. The result is reduced risk for the company, with a long-range view. There are a multitude of possible creative solutions, but the most critical part of this process is the process itself—not as much what we do, but *how* we do it.

There is certainly no way that a company can (or should) take care of all of an ex-employee's needs after the separation, but there may be some specific actions that can be accomplished to make this transition easier, if considered carefully and thoughtfully. Financial rewards do not have to be the solution, as the above case illustrates to some degree. Sometimes it is just a matter of someone (preferably someone outside of the company) who can help direct this individual to existing community services. Sometimes it is only a matter of treating this person in a fair and respectful manner and finding ways to help him or her exit with dignity intact.

There are costs to this approach. In the above example, the company paid for the services of the threat assessment professional, continued this employee for another three weeks under the disability program, paid for a month of outplacement counseling, and assumed the bill for a couple of months of COBRA insurance coverage. However, this was indeed a situation that was assessed as high-risk, which in this case meant that if termination had proceeded as planned, this employee and maybe a supervisor or two might be dead.

Even if the employer had attempted to prevent this outcome through a standard process, such as retaining security, that would only have addressed the company's safety until he was escorted off the premises, and probably would not have prevented his suicide, with all the extended consequences of that. At what point could the company feel safe enough to dismiss the extra security? And how would they know? And when would the supervisor begin to sleep through the night without getting up to nervously investigate every sound in the night?

There are costs incurred with a proactive approach, but they are typically quite minimal when compared to the consequences of inaction. Particularly traumatic is when a company and its employees are held virtually hostage by a pervasive fear of the unknown, wondering where he is and when they will see him again.

Threat Assessment at Termination

While threat assessment involves engaging the employee in an interactive process (sometimes over an extended period), the termination session itself should be a relatively brief meeting. This is not the time to discuss or rehash past issues and concerns with the employee, but to present the company's decision in a way that leaves no room for negotiation or discussion. As noted above, separation should be complete and final; doors should be closed, not opened.

Generally, risk assessment occurs before the day of termination, giving the company time to develop and prepare an appropriate strategy. If there is a need for an assessment and/or intervention to occur during the actual termination, clearly separating this intervention from the termination itself is recommended. While there are a variety of possible approaches, we typically prefer in these cases to have the employer conduct the termination session with the employee first. This usually involves the manager (generally not the immediate supervisor) and one other (typically a human resource representative). This is usually a very brief session that is relatively scripted. The employee is informed of the company's decision, followed by a brief review of any conditions or benefits that may be included.

The employee is then asked to speak to the company's external consultant, who is standing by. It can be explained that the consultant was summoned in order to conduct an interview and an on-site review due to the company's concerns about circumstances pertaining to the employee and consequences of the separation process. At that point, the threat assessment consultant is introduced to the employee, who will further explain his or her role and who then conducts the appropriate interview, after the other parties leave the room.

This interview can serve several goals:

1. Its *primary intent* is to allow a trained threat assessment professional the opportunity to conduct an interview with the subject, at a critical moment, in order to achieve a better understanding of any *risk-related factors* which should be considered in any subsequent intervention process.

2. It allows the consultant to identify any particular *needs or issues* that may also be critical to the success and safety of the termination process. Hopefully, there will be relatively few surprises in this area if a thorough preliminary assessment has been accomplished before this meeting; however, there are—more often than not—new issues that arise or old ones that require clarification.

3. It *introduces the consultant* to the individual, as someone who is external to the company and who may be able to facilitate whatever may be deemed necessary to the process. If further intervention in required, the company may want to utilize the services of this consultant to reach

out to this particular individual, which will be more easily accomplished since the ex-employee is now familiar with the consultant and his or her role. This intervention can occur on an as-needed basis, if the ex-employee becomes somehow unstable and begins making threats, for example, or it may occur as part of a planned monitoring and management process that was established during termination.

4. The assessment consultant may also identify the *need for other resources*. The above-mentioned case serves as an example, when the employee appears to be suicidal, in which case the company may have to take a relatively active role in getting the individual to a hospital, contacting the family, and so forth.

5. Finally, the participation of an external consultant can help *identify any organizational issues* that were revealed by this termination that may suggest a need for some kind of internal review.

The employee may emerge from the initial meeting emotionally distraught and/or somewhat numbed by the news. At this point, the consultant has the opportunity to assess the subject's emotional status and allow him or her to emotionally stabilize sufficiently to safely exit the building. If the consultant believes that there are issues of safety in terms of the employee either hurting him- or herself or others, then this is an opportunity to identify and alert appropriate community-based services, law enforcement agencies, and such.

This interview provides the consultant with a chance to ascertain whether there exist probable future problems that can be immediately addressed through some kind of creative action by the employer before the individual exits. In the example mentioned earlier, the consultant may only now learn of the health problems in the employee's family and their concerns about insurance coverage. In this case, the consultant can quickly caucus with the team after the interview, in order to determine whether something can be built into the separation process that can facilitate a safer and friendlier conclusion, such as agreeing to extend the employee's insurance coverage.

It has been our continuing experience that if the threat assessment professional conducts and presents him- or herself in a fair and respectful manner and has experience in working with angry people in critical situations, then there is a good chance that this individual will be able to engage in a relatively productive interaction. Certainly, it again needs to be stated that the consultant is an agent of the company and cannot counsel the individual; the situation often requires that the consultant needs to continually remind the employee of that fact, as the just-separated employee can be quite emotionally needy. The consultant's primary role is always threat assessment and management, and any attempt to influence is in the interest of safety.

If the employee requires emotional or other support, then the consultant can help arrange and facilitate the appropriate referral. If there are any difficulties in the individual's ability to pursue that or other resources, then perhaps the company or the consultant can help the employee find ways to remove those barriers. This may be as simple as extending the company's EAP services and locating a phone number. If the individual wants to exit the session, call his or her attorney, or refuse to continue, then the consultant will not, under any circumstances, argue or attempt to dissuade this decision.

At the conclusion of this interview, the employee meets again with the company's managers to clarify and finalize some of the procedural and logistic issues, and proceeds with the exiting arrangement. Before this final meeting, the consultant will usually want to caucus with the managers, in order to prep them as to issues that may be of concern and relevant to this final meeting. These may include some ideas about the exiting strategy. Prior to all of this, the team will be already aware of potential issues and will be prepared for a range of possible outcomes.

After the final session, a relatively short debriefing should again occur, in order to determine whether there should be any changes in the exit procedures. At the conclusion of the termination sessions, and after the employee has left, the team will then conduct a more extensive debriefing, at which time they will discuss the follow-up process.

The Logistics of the Termination Process

As has been our mantra throughout this book, careful pre-planning is essential to a safe and successful process, and nowhere is this more important than when preparing for an employee's termination. Not only is this an inherently difficult interaction, but it may also represent our last opportunity to influence an event that has potential long-range implications.

Consideration must be given to factors such as the timing, the script, and the physical setting, among other concerns. If the company has reason to believe that the employee may be dangerous and may have a weapon in his possession, or in a briefcase, or out in his vehicle, then they have to be prepared for all the possibilities that could occur if this is indeed the case. Each and every step of the termination process should include an examination of all the different ways in which the situation could go awry and place others in danger. This includes if and where security should be located, the positions of other participants in the termination session, the location of the meeting in the building (or even outside of the workplace), the specific exit route, parking lot security issues, and so forth. The company's internal security or its external security consultant should be actively involved in each and every stage of the planning and implementation processes.

There has been a great deal of discussion about which day is best to terminate an individual. It has been recommended by some that this should be accomplished on a Friday; since most people do not work on weekends, this will be experienced as less dissonant and traumatizing. I am not of the opinion that Friday terminations are always that beneficial. The weekends are a relatively unstructured time, and members of the community or family may not be as available; their whereabouts may not be as predictable. It is also very difficult for the ex-employee to begin engaging in job searches or any other purposeful activities, such as meeting with outplacement counselors. The individual may also engage in some behaviors, including substance abuse, which may further destabilize the situation to some degree. While the typical structure of work may be gone, there is virtually no structure during the weekend, such that it may serve to increase stress. Timing, in terms of the days of the week, is generally not that important, but we generally prefer mid-week. Monday—a day that appears to be inherently stressful for many—is generally never recommended.

In terms of where to conduct the termination session, this should be in a more neutral setting, and not the supervisor's office, which may have a great deal of association for the employee. The supervisor's office may elicit many feelings regarding authority and past interactions with that supervisor (or other supervisors), and may actually increase the risk to that supervisor, by virtue of this association. I believe that it should occur as close to the exit as possible, and should have a minimal amount of furniture or items that can be used in case the individual does become disruptive.

Those who are conducting the termination session should sit closer to the door, to facilitate a quick exit. Security personnel should be stationed in an adjoining office or very close by, and everyone should understand the procedure involved if there is a decision to alert security. There are many devices that can be purchased at the local Radio Shack store (including wireless doorbells) that can be utilized. (Based on past experiences, it is highly recommended that the activating device not be placed in a pocket, such that it can be accidentally engaged by sitting on it, for example. Having security personnel burst in unexpectedly in an otherwise stable termination session can be, needless to say, embarrassing, highly disruptive, and difficult to explain.) Security professionals should generally be in plain clothes or at least not be obtrusive in any manner. It is generally recommended that off-duty police officers be utilized, since they have the power to arrest that particular individual if his or her behavior warrants it.

In terms of who should conduct the meeting, it generally should not be just the supervisor and in most situations, should not be the immediate supervisor at all. We do not want to raise the risk of harm toward the supervisor in associating him or her with this action. Further, having the supervisor there will raise the probability that the subject will attempt to rehash old issues. Additionally, that relationship may have deteriorated to the point that it may be too much of a challenge to the supervisor's patience. Preferably, it should be someone at a level above the supervisor, and it should be someone with experience with difficult terminations. Typically, these terminations should include a manager and a human resource representative.

There are sometimes concerns that the employee will be offended and angered that the supervisor was not personally involved—that he "wasn't man enough to face me." Sometimes, the supervisors themselves feel equally derelict if they do not confront the employee directly. In normal circumstances, this may make sense. However, if we have an employee who is identified as being potentially harmful, especially to his or her supervisor, I am less concerned about whether we have somehow offended this employee by not giving that person another chance to challenge the supervisor. Once the situation involves a potential risk of violence, our concerns are at a different level.

Generally, I recommend that the manager not "beat around the bush," and that they give notice that the individual is terminated in the first sentence or two. Statements should be direct, unambiguous, and spoken very clearly without a great deal of detail. It must be remembered that someone who hears this for the first time may initially undergo enough emotional shock that he or she will not be functioning mentally anywhere near the normal level. He or she is not likely to hear everything accurately and will not be able to mentally process much in the way of detailed or complicated information. This is why we will often have the HR representative explain some of the details about benefits and such in a second session, after the meeting with the threat assessment specialist.

Once the termination is completed, the employee leaves the

building under a previously planned process. Obviously, revoking access control cards, company credit cards, keys, and sensitive company information is part of this process. It is generally not advisable to allow the individual to return to his or her office. In particular, the ex-employee should not be allowed on the company's computer, as there is often sensitive information that could be damaged or stolen. Escorting the individual through the workplace back to his or her office can be very embarrassing and is not recommended. We have generally found that if separated employees need something at that moment from their office, it can be identified and someone can retrieve it for them. They can be allowed back in the office after hours under supervision in order to retrieve the rest of their belongings, or simply have these shipped to them.

Besides revoking access to the building, the team needs to consider whether to place a BOLO (Be On the Lookout) notice. All critical employees (security and otherwise) who may encounter the employee at the entrances (including the parking lot) need to be aware of this individual, have a photograph, and be aware of the car that he or she drives. Certainly if there is any change in the front desk or security staff, even months after the termination, the new staff members should be similarly advised.

If this is an individual who has made or posed a threat against anyone in particular, then the team should determine its obligations to warn or otherwise address the safety concerns of those individuals. There exists a range of options available, from providing extra security to invoking legal action (i.e., protective orders) to temporary relocation. It is not the intent of this chapter to address all the security-related measures that can be invoked as part of this process. Security requirements can vary tremendously and require the input of trained security advisors.

Finally, the terminated employee should be provided with the name of a specific contact. This should ideally be no more than one employee, usually in human resources, along with the name of the company's external consultant if so involved. Many organizations that utilize a threat assessment consultant during termination decide to have this consultant as the only contact, and this has proven to work very well. As noted above, we nearly always recommend at least a follow-up phone call by the company's consultant and not by the company, unless it is someone who is perceived to be outside the specific context of the termination.

If outplacement counseling is included as part of the separation package, it is highly recommended that the outplacement counselor be there at termination to meet with this individual before the termination is concluded. Terminated employees may not understand the value of outplacement and sometimes may be reluctant to call. Even if the outplacement counselor is not present, it is recommended that the assigned counselor telephone the individual afterwards or that the consultant remind the ex-employee of the outplacement services and encourage that contact.

On the issue of whether to allow the person back into the workplace, this is rarely advised. While we would all ideally like for that individual to be able to return, visit with old friends and coworkers, and have a chance to "work through" this transition, this rarely works to anyone's benefit. In the case of employment terminations, this is a Band-Aid that generally needs to be removed quickly, in order to expedite the recovery process for everyone.

By allowing the ex-employee to return to the workplace, the company is at risk of witnessing a range of emotional reactions that can be embarrassing, awkward, or disruptive, with little opportunity for any kind of true "closure." The relationship between an individual and an employer (and other employees) is a unique one that cannot be regained or even redefined in any useful way. Further, the employees who remain and who are still actively engaged in their employment are hardly in a position to effectively help that individual in any useful manner through this transition process. Further, it is difficult to imagine any benefit that the remaining employees could experience from these visits.

In conclusion...

The separation process is never easy. With employees

identified as presenting a risk of harm, the company must proceed in a careful and considered manner. The eventual goal should always be not just to survive the process, but to orchestrate it in such a way that the subject employee can exit with a belief that it was conducted in a fair and respectful manner.

While the company has no legal obligation to help, it may want to be cognizant of those ex-employees who may not have the skills or resources to easily recover from the experience. If the company acts in a responsible and considerate manner, with an eye to the long-term needs of that employee, it generally proves beneficial for everyone. The separated employee is able to more effectively move on with his or her life; the company's employees are less apt to be looking over their shoulders as they exit the parking lot; and society as a whole is better served if there is one less angry and wounded citizen walking the streets, bent on revenge.

Chapter 7

Defusing Angry Employees
A Manager's Guide to Crisis & Conflict Resolution

Every supervisor has to, at some time or another, confront the angry and aggrieved employee. These may be employees under stress or who feel somehow mistreated by the organization or other members of the organization. This may be a customer or client who feels traumatized by a particular grievance or perceived wrong. This could be part of an ongoing conflict between two employees who have locked horns in a lasting and presumably irresolvable struggle. Or it could be an employee or a customer with whom communication is a chronically difficult experience.

In high-risk situations involving a potential for violence, supervisors find themselves on the front line, having to engage and defuse before there is time to call in support. As previously noted, many incidents involving a threat of violence occur following a long period of incubation, which have been nurtured by a general reluctance to confront the issues. Supervisors and the subject's coworkers often lack the confidence to confront these early grievances and conflicts without the risk of antagonizing the individual to a dangerous and uncontrollable level. Both major and minor conflicts and disagreements are therefore avoided, instead of being addressed directly, and simply wait for another day.

Granted, in the grand scheme of things, some conflicts seem irresolvable, and some individuals are best avoided—at least, that's what our survival instincts may tell us when having to face these situations. However, simply detaching ourselves from the relationship offers no real solution when we have to work with or supervise this individual on a daily basis. Many issues and most conflicts do not just solve themselves over time.

This chapter is offered as a practical guide to supervisors and managers, and essentially anyone who has to engage and interact with angry individuals in potentially explosive situations—which includes many of us at some point in our lives. In fact, you will find these techniques useful in most of your social interactions, as these are often extensions of basic principles that are being discovered by different professionals who work in a variety of disciplines from marital therapy to hostage negotiation.

The Principles of Crisis/Conflict Negotiation

The art and science of negotiating with individuals in conflict and in emotionally charged circumstances is a relatively recent study, but there are some basic principles that are consistently emerging that are becoming widely accepted. If one reviews the literature on hostage negotiation, dispute resolution, and even marital therapy, for example, one discovers many of the same concepts, albeit expressed with different terminology and utilized for different purposes. Many of the techniques that we will be discussing here are techniques that can actually be of use within *any* relationship that could potentially involve angry conflict. The exciting result of our current level of understanding is that we now generally *know what works!*

This area, which I refer to here as "crisis negotiation," is relatively unique in that it is typically a relatively delicate process, in which an inappropriate action or choice of words could escalate the situation quickly, with little chance for redemption. There is far less opportunity for error. The same principles that are used in any kind of negotiation are applicable in these events, but these incidents often require an approach that is more cautious and intentional.

Most of what is presented here is based on what I have learned though experience, as is the case with most who have been involved in this kind of work before there was much in the way of formal instruction (which remains largely the case). This represents what has worked for me, which is generally very consistent with what others have been discovering. Again, the literature has recently produced some guidelines for procedures that are remarkably consistent and have been largely validated.

I want to refer the reader to Fisher and Ury's (1991) excellent landmark work in this area, that helped to lay the foundation for much of this and has probably provided some of the terminology that has now become standard in this area.

The Steps in Conflict Resolution

There are essentially three goals that we are attempting to accomplish when negotiating in difficult and high-risk circumstances. Our goals will be to:

A. De-escalate: to reduce the level of emotional pressure that has come to bear on the issue, so that the parties can think and act more rationally, less defensively, and with less ego investment.

B. Reframe: to identify the "real" or underlying needs beneath the issues and redefine the problem to a more workable format, so that we can effectively…

C. Problem-solve: to move the relationship to a problem-solving mode, where all parties are engaged and even allied in a process of resolving problems, as opposed to simply attacking each other.

All the techniques offered here would be serving one or more of these three goals. There is a great deal of overlap, and these three goals are not mutually exclusive, nor do they necessarily occur by means of a linear process.

The Win-Win Solution

This is not just about how to "talk someone down." It is not usually sufficient to "defuse" an individual for the short-term goal of re-establishing safety or stability, by simply applying some emotional Band-Aids and sending the person on his or her way. We want the other party to walk away and not come to the conclusion down the road that he or she has somehow been deceived or short-changed in any way. We want that person to be able to fully disengage, with satisfaction and a belief that he or she achieved some degree of resolution—in which the person has "won," or at least has not "lost."

Are we over-reaching by discussing conflict resolution when all that any supervisor may wish to achieve is just to calm everyone down long enough to bring in other resources? If the reader is a supervisor or a member of a security team, you may be saying at this point, "It's not my job to negotiate with people and help them get their needs met or resolve their conflicts. It's my job to keep the peace and keep them from hurting each other. It's up to others to address their needs or resolve their problems." As I hope will become obvious, the techniques of defusing or calming angry people are the same ones that ultimately serve to elucidate the individual's interests, which in turn, rather naturally lays the foundation for a real resolution.

Conversely, the skills that we use to resolve disputes are often the best skills to utilize in the de-escalation process. Identifying underlying needs and engaging the individual in a problem-solving process will also serve to reduce the level of emotional intensity. Resolving an issue that is important to the subject is what most of us accomplish when we attempt to stabilize situations. This does not mean that we resolve the issue as initially presented by the parties involved, but we may actually resolve more critical and fundamental issues, such as their need to be heard and treated fairly, for example. This is a topic that will hopefully become more obvious as we proceed though this subject.

When those in the area of dispute resolution use the term "win-win," it is not meant to imply that all parties achieve their original demands. But the fact that they may not achieve their initial interests does not therefore imply that they necessarily receive something less! As we proceed through a discussion of this area, I hope that it will become obvious that a critical ingredient in this process is the negotiator's ability to identify the demanding individual's primary interests, such that some sort of resolution occurs—that may actually speak *more* directly to the individual's primary interests than did his or her original demands.

Controlling Natural Responses

Negotiating in critical, high-risk situations oftentimes requires quick but well-considered decisions, which sounds like a contradiction—and to some degree it is. The negotiator must remain conscious of the other party and the effect of the negotiator's communication on the other party, intended or otherwise. It must be an intentional process, one that requires self-discipline and attention. An inappropriate remark can divert the process and risk losing the relationship, with critical consequences. The negotiator must not only remain keenly aware of the other party, but also him- or herself.

The negotiator must first of all be aware and always cognizant of those reactions that will naturally occur if not carefully monitored and inhibited. These naturally occur by the shear fact that we are human. We all respond to dangerous situations in certain, pre-programmed ways, thanks to the evolution of our genetic makeup. The natural response that we generally utilize in many dangerous situations has been referred to as the "fight or flight" reaction. We more specifically react to angry or particularly aggressive behavior in others in also rather predictable ways and for the same reasons.

As first described by William Ury (1993), we can be generally assured that we will most likely respond to aggressive behavior in one of the three following ways:

1. Fighting back
2. Giving in
3. Terminating the relationship.

We consistently utilize these three natural responses because they work! They help us to effectively rid ourselves of this relationship that we perceive to be threatening and uncomfortable at the least. However, we may not have the luxury of following these natural instincts. We may have an investment in maintaining this presently disagreeable relationship, due to other long-term goals—or it may just be part of the job.

The first and foremost task for managers in these situations is to remain aware of and to *harness their normal reactions*.

Each of these three responses may periodically emerge throughout the interaction to undermine the negotiation process. While we may not actually attempt to physically strike another person, we may find ourselves *"getting back"* by a host of more subtle responses that reflect a process of one-upmanship, perhaps utilizing a sarcastic or condescending remark. The response of *giving in* may occur in the workplace when an intimidating employee is allowed to engage in behavior without consequences, as a passive response to avoid the consequences that confrontation may bring. Finally, we can *terminate the relationship* in a variety of ways. In the workplace, we may simply transfer the employee to another department. We may even "eliminate" the problem employee's position, as a way of ridding ourselves of this relationship without having to confront the real concern.

As negotiators, we may also seek to prematurely end the relationship by trying to solve the problem too quickly, before we have undergone steps that are critical to the resolution process. This represents a form of avoidance that may not be conscious and is particularly dangerous because it may lead to a false sense of relief, which is eventually disrupted without warning when the real issue resurfaces.

It will be continually beneficial to remind ourselves that a person who is angry beyond reason is looking for a better reason to be angry. He or she may be looking for someone to represent an antagonist, who can in turn absorb and justify this rage. Our most fundamental job is to harness our tendency to react and to not provide the other individual with any more reasons to be angry. We have to avoid the trap of becoming the enemy.

Knowing our own weaknesses and "hot buttons" is a critical part of this process. We cannot take attacks personally, although that may be precisely the way that they were intended. A good negotiator has to find some way to suspend his or her ego and to place the impulse to defend oneself on hold. We must find an internal dialogue that allows us to refrain the subject's behavior differently, such that our defenses do not become engaged.

Before we proceed further, it goes without saying that there are times when one actually *should* follow one's instincts. If you believe that your life and safety are indeed endangered, maintaining the relationship may no longer be an immediate goal, and one of these natural responses (i.e., running away) may be a much more appropriate response, in order to ensure your survival (which is always a primary goal).

Techniques of De-escalation

In any kind of critical negotiation process, one cannot discuss the presented issues effectively without engaging in what has been variously referred to as a defusing, de-escalation, or disarming process. One cannot reason with or even attempt to resolve issues with someone who literally cannot be receptive, due to his or her emotional status.

This will all have to be accomplished in the face of insistent demands and pressure to instantly address the person's grievances. However, if you attempt to resolve the issues too early in the process, you will very quickly discover that the other party is not prepared to accept the solution, even if it appears indeed to be a viable solution. Despite what the insistent party may assert, there are generally more fundamental issues that have to be addressed, before that person will able to "turn down the volume" enough to engage in a reasonable interactive process.

In the end, it is often not so much *what* we do in the process of crisis negotiation but *how* we do it. The manner in which we conduct the process (and ourselves within the process) often matters more in the final analysis than what the aggrieved party may or may not ultimately receive, in terms of tangible rewards. In many negotiations of this nature, the individual will walk away with a sufficient degree of satisfaction, but without any of the demands that were initially presented, because the *process itself* satisfied his or her primary interests. Under this topic of de-escalation, we will be focusing on the following nine fundamental principles and specific techniques.

Acknowledge concerns

After harnessing natural reactions, the most useful and fundamental step in any kind of defusing or negotiation process relies on the negotiator's ability to recognize and verbally acknowledge the other party's concerns. This is a necessary and primary part of the process that cannot be short-circuited.

Most of those in conflict want, more than anything else, to know that they are being heard and that their concerns have been understood, or at least recognized. Many times, this may be so fundamental that it is in actuality, more important than winning demands, regardless of initial assertions. I have personally been involved in countless negotiations and mediations that have been successful largely due to this single accomplishment: that the other parties understood and gave a "serious listen" to each other's issues.

Sometimes when introducing myself to an angry, demanding employee, I will very early include a statement that underscores my understanding that they believe that they have been "treated unfairly"—which nearly always resides at the core of their rage, regardless of the particular circumstances. I will literally begin the conversation with the statement, "My name is Dr. McElhaney. The company has informed me that you feel that you have been unfairly treated and has asked that I review your concerns." This is an easy assumption, and it is this simple recognition of that fact which alerts the other party that I am *already* listening to him or her. That recognition alone can set the tone and will cause an immediate reduction in the emotional pressure. The individual with whom you are negotiating has to *know* that he or she is being heard; that person will not decrease the volume until this has been satisfied.

This does not imply that negotiators have to agree with the other party's allegations or viewpoints, but you have to at least acknowledge the other's experience. As we will discuss, you are also allowing the employee a chance to sort out and understand his or her own experience. As noted above, you will find that you may be pulled to debate the validity of the other's experience, but this is not the time, if it ever is. You may likewise find yourself wanting to be defensive and to strike back when the other party alleges, for example, that the negotiator is part of this unfairness. It is easy and natural to respond to an allegation of unfairness with a defensive "I am not!" or "How can you say that after all I've done?" You should not directly disagree with this individual's perception of his or her own experience in this phase of the process—and should do so only when a rapport has been developed that is based on the other party's satisfaction that you indeed are listening.

Acknowledging subjects' feelings, as opposed to content, is the stuff of the early phases of this process. This is the case even if you believe that their experience of an event is a result of misinterpretation or misinformation, which may (or may not) be something that can be addressed later when they are better able to consider these issues reasonably. Often subjects will ask for some sort of validation, such as, "You know you'd feel angry too if this happened to you." At these points, it would be generally advantageous for you to acknowledge that "Yes, I would be angry too if someone treated me unfairly." Whether or not you actually empathize or even understand their reactions is not important. You are simply trying to normalize their experience for them and to reassure them that you are not dismissive or critical and that you are attempting to understand their experience.

Affirm the person

Not only is it important to acknowledge the other party's experience, but you also need to acknowledge his or her individual worth. This often will feel unnecessary or even contraindicated. Those who are enraged or abusive may appear cocky and self-satisfied to a fault, when it is actually more often than not, quite the reverse. What you are witnessing are generally not the behaviors of the self-confident. These individuals may be struggling to maintain some degree of self-respect, and they may have difficulty moving to a more productive level until they find a way to regain that. *You* are the one who must help them with that struggle.

Acknowledge their expertise and affirm their goodness, even though your instincts may prompt you otherwise. In battle, we attempt to appear powerful to our antagonist and will in turn attempt to cut him down to size at every opportunity. In negotiation, you may have to bolster the self-esteem in a person who appears to already have an ample supply. Before the other party is able to relinquish his or her aggressive posture and treat you with respect, he or she has to feel some degree of self-respect. You will have to aid with that process, so that he or she will eventually become less defensive and less threatened.

Toss in compliments whenever you get the chance. If he is defending his work performance, affirm his value in that area. If she begins discussing her financial obligations to her family, take that as an opportunity to acknowledge that she indeed appears to be a committed parent. Whether the subject is or is not a good employee or a committed parent is not our concern. What is critical is that we help to reduce their defensiveness by communicating that we are not here to sit in judgment, to criticize or to otherwise diminish their sense of worth in any way. I will also use this opportunity to set expectations that I would like for them to meet, i.e., "Joe, I know that you are a hard worker and a good person, and I am sure that we can work through this in a reasonable manner."

Try to remember throughout this process that even the most intimidating—contrary to appearance—are not working from a position of strength. Most people become enraged and aggressive because they are threatened, abused or unfairly treated. Despite appearances, they are likely experiencing a feeling of powerlessness. While it appears contrary and even illogical, we are seeking ultimately to help *empower them*. Only when the other party feels more empowered is he or she able lay down the weapons and consider more reasonable options.

Allow some venting

Be careful not to get to the issues and the solution too quickly. Everyone needs time to "have their say." Negotiating is not so much about talking as it is about listening. The best and most effective negotiators, in my experience, are those who know how to listen and generally do relatively little talking.

Avoid the tendency to want to give them an answer or to respond to their comments with a solution. That will come much later, if at all. Sit back. Be patient. You need to understand their world. The more they vent, the more material you have to work with. Encourage the conversation with nods and affirmations. Show them that you are listening. Use this time to figure them out.

There may come a time when you have to interrupt if an incessant monologue develops. They may eventually need help redirecting their energy to more productive goals. At that point, you will become more active, but this comes later. Initially, the other party at the very least needs to *know* that he or she is heard.

Be respectful in manner

Regardless of the other party's behavior, avoid the tendency to respond in a similar manner. Maintain a respectful attitude, always. We tend to mirror and follow each other's lead in our interactions. In situations involving conflict, the natural tendency is to attack in a response to someone's attack. If he ignores you, then you will respond by ignoring him. If he disagrees with you, you will disagree with him, and so forth.

The goal is to reverse his or her tactics or approach. You want to counter the other person's behavior with a respectful and considerate response. Stephen Covey (1989) says in his book, "to be understood, seek first to understand," a rule that remains applicable throughout all of our social interactions. If you want them to listen to you, you must first listen to them. If you want them to acknowledge your point, you must first acknowledge theirs. To get them to agree with you, you must start by agreeing with them. Set the tone that you wish for them to mirror. Your behavior says, "I am going to be respectful to you and I am expecting you to act the same." You set expectations by your approach.

Adopt an "open," nonaggressive physical presence

Your physical presentation will speak volumes, and it should be consistent with your message. In order to reduce the other party's sense of threat, be careful that you do indeed present a nonthreatening physical demeanor.

Speak with your hands open and avoid physical gestures that are aggressive, such as pointing your finger or clenching your fist. Folding your arms is also defensive and often interpreted as a lack of interest, or that you are ignoring the subject. Give the other party plenty of physical space, and above all, make sure that you are positioned such that he or she does not feel trapped. Keep your voice tone, volume, pitch, and speed lower than the other person's, and slowly bring it down.

Find areas of agreement: say "yes"

The natural tendency, when someone presents a list of demands, is to skip over the issues on which we agree and proceed to the area of disagreement. In confrontational interactions, the other party is anticipating a challenge, that you will say "no," and will prepare his or her defenses accordingly. Offer instead a "yes."

Find something to agree with, and ignore the areas of disagreement initially. Continue with that approach and continue to find areas of agreement, such that it will begin to facilitate a redefinition of the relationship. If you cannot find topics of agreement, discuss the weather or last night's ball game if you have to. Find some kind of common ground. Finding areas of agreement and opportunities to say "yes" will set the stage and reinforce a process that will increase the probability of further agreement. Find ways also that he or she can agree with you. Make it easier for the other person also to say "yes."

Avoid "yes, but...," which is not a "yes" and generally is emotionally perceived as a "no." You can actually see parties in conflict stiffen when we insert that "but" after the initial affirmation. Try using "yes, and" instead of "yes, but." Compare, for example: "Yes, Bob, I understand your need for a bigger office, *but* I have a lot to consider" to "Yes, Bob, I understand your need for a bigger office, *and* I have a lot to consider." The latter does not feel like a dismissal or rejection, whereas the former can be experienced as such.

Avoid rejecting anything outright. Like a strong wind, going head-on into their demands is usually not productive As we'll discuss in the next section, you want to eventually have them come to their own conclusion that it was not a good idea (or that there are better solutions) without you having to make it a battleground. It is generally better to ignore demands or any attempts to establish firm positions.

Avoid "you" statements

Use "I" whenever possible, to discuss your experience, as opposed to the more accusatory "you." The use of "you," especially as the initial word in the sentence, is often considered to be an aggressive word, as that is precisely how it is often used. Referring to your own experience is a disarming technique, which feels less confrontational. Again, compare the relative difference between "Sam, *you* need to lower your voice. *You*'re being too intimidating" to "Sam, *I* feel intimidated when you speak in that manner." The former will more likely engender a defensive response, while the latter will give the other party an opportunity to regard you, and perhaps respond to you, in a more considerate manner.

Offer apologies

Another disarming technique is, very simply, to apologize. This need not be meek or self-blaming. You can at the least apologize for your share. I often go beyond that and even apologize for events that may to any rational thinking, be actually far outside what I can control. It's relatively painless and it puts the other off guard. Further, it sends the message that you are willing and not afraid to expose your own vulnerability. This is, of course, against the natural reaction to be self-protective in the face of their accusations. This again undermines any attempt to fight any unnecessary battles and encourage an antagonistic relationship.

Ignore/deflect attacks

You must ignore and deflect the other party's attacks. These are usually delivered—consciously or not—to create an antagonistic relationship. Step to the side and allow their occurrence without reaction. Similarly, ignore demands, especially those that include deadlines. Many of these attacks and demands are often offered as a challenge or to cause a reaction or to create conflict. Do not take them personally—even though that may be how they were intended—and respond to them only when it is to your advantage.

One way of deflecting an attack is to reframe it—a personal attack as friendly. Even if someone says for example, "I'd watch your back if I were you," your response can be, "I appreciate your concern, and I'd like to discuss that later with you, but right now I'd like to understand your concerns." Even if that statement indeed represents a serious threat, you do not have to respond to it on the other person's timetable. Do not give the other party the power of controlling the conversation by these means. This does not imply that we should internally dismiss the statement as somehow not a valid concern. This kind of threat may remain a concern that may require a response at the appropriate time. You may decide to return to that issue later: "Joe, before we finish up, I need to ask you about something that you said earlier to me, that is of concern." Note here who is now controlling the tone and content of the conversation. Your decision not to verbally respond to attacks does not imply that you do not remain conscious of their implications.

Needs Identification and Reframing

People come into conflict with a notion of what they want—a list of desires, demands, positions, and/or grievances, presented with intensity and passion. Underlying each of these stated goals are more fundamental needs and interests, which the desired goal represents or seeks to fulfill. We, more often than not, may have relatively little or no awareness or understanding of these underlying needs. Our desire for a new car, a week at the beach, or a million dollars may represent needs for stimulation, relaxation, security, etc., which may or may not be satisfied by these fantasies. In fact, once the underlying needs are better understood, other equally (or more) satisfying options may emerge.

To arrive at a true resolution, you have to ultimately reframe the stated demands and positions in a way that provides us with not just more available options, but generally better ones—ones that are actually in our best interests. If for no other reason, you generally cannot meet their demands as presented anyway. By identifying the underlying interests, other options will literally emerge that will sometimes reveal a solution that is far more satisfactory to these interests than the original demand. This is how we arrive at a "win-win."

Your job is to not only discover and identify these underlying issues, but to also involve the other party in that process. You are not only educating yourself about these underlying issues, but you are educating the other party, who may be equally clueless.

You and the other party, consciously or not, are mutually involved in a learning process.

The corner office

Bob and Susan are fighting over the recently vacated corner office, the one with all the windows. Bill, the manager, has ignored their demands so long that Bob and Susan have now each increased their volume and are openly fighting over the issue, causing other problems within the workplace. Bill feels compelled by their incessant demands to make a decision—to choose one of them to occupy that office, and face the other's anger and disappointment.

Bill is reluctant to discuss the issue with either, believing that it represents an irresolvable problem, along with the fact that Bill believes that he already understands the dynamics involved well enough. After all, all employees prefer the status and benefits of the big corner office. It's an age-old problem, and he would just as soon avoid the aggravation of hearing their predictable demands and complaints. However, having just completed a course in conflict resolution, Bill decided to give each of them a hearing, utilizing his newly-acquired "active listening" skills.

An interview with Bob (a very long-term employee) surfaced Bob's longstanding belief that he has received relatively inadequate acknowledgement or reward, during his 27 years of commitment to the company. He had been rather passive in the past but had decided that it was time that the company gave him what he perceived as his "due." Moving him to the larger office represented at least a "token" of recognition, after years of perceived neglect. In fact, Bob's complaints revealed to Bill that he had indeed been slighted and had failed to receive some of the benefits that he was due, based on his work on a recent project. Bill agrees with Bob that he has been slighted in the past and is able to address these issues with Bob, eventually to Bob's satisfaction. Bob voluntarily approaches Bill later, stating that he has decided that he really does not want the new office, as he came to the conclusion that he is essentially comfortable with the one that he has occupied for over 20 years.

Susan, in her interview, reminded Bill that she suffers from Seasonal Affective Disorder (SAD), which has caused her to take a great deal of sick leave and has subsequently affected her productivity and overall health. She explained that SAD is a psychiatric/medical condition that causes depression in certain individuals when deprived of an adequate amount of sunlight. She is angry that the company, while having knowledge of her condition, has not stepped up and provided her with an office that is better lit. While she is insistent that the corner office is the only solution to her unique health needs, she also acknowledges during the course of the interview that she will miss her friends and coworkers if she moves, and that the move will require that she commute frequently between floors. After some investigation, Bill was able to reshuffle some offices in her present location to satisfy her needs both for more light and proximity to her staff, a solution that Susan found to be more satisfactory.

If Bill had given in to either Bob or Susan's demands as presented, by allowing one of them to move into the corner office, he would have actually committed two mistakes, because *neither* Bob nor Susan would have been truly satisfied. Both Bob and Susan seemed to hold similar and incompatible positions: that they each *had to have* the corner office. In this rather simple example (that actually occurred quite recently), Bob and Susan maintained their demands because they believed that this (moving to this office) represented their best (and only) available option. Only through an engagement in the above-mentioned interactive process were their underlying needs identified. Once identified, other solutions were generated that, in retrospect now quite obvious, such that both were satisfied with the result. Ironically, the office remained vacant. Bill was able to achieve a true "win-win" and avoid a "win-lose" (actually a "lose-lose," since the corner office did not truly offer the best alternative for either party).

Active listening

What gets us to this point is what is called "active listening"—a critical term that is utilized in an increasing variety of relationship training programs. The process of needs identification and re-framing requires that you listen well enough, in order to solicit the information that will help *both* you and the other party understand the underlying critical interests. As outlined below, this involves an active, not a passive, process on the listener's part, that seeks to eventually engage the other party in a mutual problem–solving process. Whether your goals are simply to calm someone down or ultimately address his or her demands, you will find that an active listening process is the primary vehicle that gets you to that end.

Repeat, question, re-question & rephrase

While the process of needs identification appears overwhelming to the novice, my advice in my workshops is simply, "Just act stupid." Act like you do not understand them and repeatedly ask for repetition and clarification. Ask them to repeat themselves, and then give them back their statements, to make sure that you have heard them correctly. Your conversations will be punctuated with phrases such as, "Let me see if I got that right. You're saying…," and "Could you give that to me one more time? I want to make sure I heard you correctly," and so forth.

Your primary goal is to reflect back to them what they are saying, to give them a chance to hear exactly what they said from an outside source, and further, to give them a chance to modify their statement if they wish. It gives them an opportunity to learn about themselves and refine their statement so that it more accurately reflects their interests. It slows down the conversation and their thoughts, facilitating a less emotional and more thoughtful reconsideration.

Your job is to also rephrase what they say in a way that may be more palatable and more reflective of their overall interests, thus widening the door through which eventual solutions could emerge. While you are reflecting content, you are—most importantly in the early stages—reflecting the feelings behind the statements. You are uncovering the source, what underlies these complaints. You want to understand!

Active listening does not judge or offer solutions. If the other party says that he wants to "kill" his supervisor, that can be duly noted, but you do not take issue with that statement at this point. It serves little purpose to lecture to him about the legal or moral consequences of this statement. Right now, it's just a statement. If you wish to understand its intent and what underlies it, then a nonthreatening, active listening approach is your best avenue. You may want to repeat that back to him and to reflect on the feeling behind that, such as "You want to kill him? Boy, you must be really angry at this guy." This allows the other party to expand on his feelings, and eventually the more critical issues, in a less defensive manner. Resist any internal or external pressure to unnecessarily offer your opinion. Not displaying your disapproval of his statement does not somehow imply that you approve of it. Remember that many of these kinds of statements may be intended as a challenge and as an effort to divert the dialogue into an antagonistic one.

As you engage in a dialogue that reveals their core interests, solutions will often become more obvious. What you choose to mirror back to the other party and the way in which you choose to paraphrase his or her statements will help guide the person to other possibilities. In our previous example, it was Bill saying to Susan, "So, what I hear you saying is that what you need, more than anything else, is an office that has more sunlight." This puts them both on a solution-oriented track and one in which the options will become more numerous and more applicable to her real needs. Bill could even follow up with a question: "Now help me to understand, Susan. Does this have to be natural sunlight or could this supplied by special full-spectrum bulbs?" This kind of exploratory questioning could open up other potential options. It will also, at the very least, demonstrate to Susan that Bill is actively attempting to understand her and her needs. Further, it facilitates a conversation in which both individuals are mutually participating as problem-solvers.

Avoid the tendency to move too quickly. Even if you come to an understanding (or have an idea for a solution), make sure that the other party gets there too. You ideally want the other party to come to his or her own conclusion, which is more convincing than if you were to propose it. This is an individual who is fighting for a sense of control and is likely to reject anything that is perceived as externally imposed.

Redirect with questions

I will use questions liberally, not only as a means to understand the other party's interests, but also as a means of controlling and managing the emotional intensity and direction. Questions often have a way of giving pause. Asking a question or even saying that you have a question will often cause the other party to put his or her monologue on pause and direct attention to you, giving you an opportunity to redirect. If nothing else, a question reminds the other party that you are interested in him or her.

I will also use questions to broaden the other person's perspective, in a way that is less threatening. "What do you think will happen if…" "How do you think others may view that?" "If you do that, do you think it will get what you want?" Allow the questions themselves to teach instead of providing answers. I ask many open-ended questions, and am careful not to feel obligated to help with their response. I will pose a general "Tell me more about that." And wait to hear how they fill that space.

The Journey to Problem-Solving: *Getting to "we"*

Your eventual goal is to redefine the nature of this relationship, from a discussion of "me" and "you" to a "we," where we are not working on "your problem" or "my problem," but rather on "our problem." We want to move to a discussion of the issues as if they are external and do not reside within either of us, that "we" together have the capacity to resolve. We want to perceive ourselves as allies in a common, or at least shared, struggle.

I believe that this essentially represents a more accurate way to view conflict in any case. We may both want the corner office, but the issue is more accurately one of physics. It is really not so much about Bob vs. Susan, but about how each of them as human beings is programmed—as we all are—to try to get their needs met in a world of limited resources (in this case, one corner office).

Much of this has to do with our approach and the language that we use. Use "we" and "us" whenever you can. Further, define the problem as an external one and in impersonal terms as often as possible. It is important in this process to *separate the people from the problem.* We want to avoid any tendency to assign blame. In fact, while I use the word "problem" here, I am very careful not to use that term to describe the subject's interests, as that word will be construed as assigning blame. If I say, "I understand that you have a problem…," I am likely to hear back, "I don't have a problem. They're the ones with the problem." I am more likely to refer their "concerns" for example.

I will sometimes assign blame to the "policy," some kind of legal or regulatory entity or an external, impersonal set of circumstances that we all know we cannot change. For example, Bill could say, "I can't believe the architects put so few windowed offices in this building." This always seems to be readily accepted, as it is easier to attribute blame to an impersonal entity that holds sway over all of us. It helps us to depersonalize the problem and it puts us all on the common ground subject to the same universe, encouraging a more united approach.

Directing to a future perspective

At this point, we want to avoid addressing past mistakes and direct the conversation to a future, solution-focused one. Now that we have allowed the parties to vent and are able through this process to react less emotionally, and are more able to reasonably problem-solve, we want to stay away from past issues of blame. Likewise, we want to focus on the positive aspects of our choices.

Ask for help

If we have been successful in reducing the emotional level and have better defined our interests, there will be opportunities to ask the other party for help during this, the problem-solving process. By asking for his or her input and help when confronting a roadblock, you demonstrate that both of you are indeed involved in a mutual process. Asking for advice or direction does not mean that you have to abide by it. The very fact that the other party feels more in control may facilitate more responsible and less egocentric decision-making, if he or she is emotionally ready to assume that role. Asking for direction can be accomplished at various points: "How can I help you with that?," "What can I do?," or better still, "What can we do about that?" Give them a chance to find a way out that they can live with.

Respect the right to choose

If overheard, there are parts of this conversation that may sound somewhat controversial. Throughout this discourse, you should do nothing to deny the other's right to make his or her own decision, even if those decisions are inappropriate, wrong, illegal, or immoral. This does not mean that you condone or allow the implementation of any such decisions. After all, you cannot ultimately control someone else's thoughts or behavior, and should not attempt to. Denying the other party the right to decide is not within your power. For example, if an employee threatens to kill his supervisor or himself, we sometimes want to immediately talk him out of that. We sometimes will even go so far as to make a statement such as, "You can't (or shouldn't) do that." This will often be perceived as a challenge, or resented as an attempt to be critical or to control him. You may actually increase the likelihood of that action.

Remember that there are many reasons that people make these statements. There are times when you may have to actively be involved in preventing a threat from being carried out, but the act of responding to these kinds of statements in a way that denies the speaker the right to make his or her own decisions is usually disrespectful and counterproductive.

Do not allow yourself to be tested or manipulated by their threats, by feeling that you have to immediately dissuade them. By initially allowing them the right to choose and to even threaten an inadvisable action, only then will you have the opportunity to explore other options. I will often respond to those threats with an acknowledgement: "Yes, you could do that." This kind of statement alerts the other individual that I will not engage in a struggle to dissuade him and that by implication, he alone will have to take responsibility for his decisions. As I mentioned previously, by actually empowering the other party, we may be more effective in reducing the chances of him acting on that threat.

In conclusion, I offer two final thoughts. First, always be prepared to think "outside the box." There are always many more solutions than are initially assumed based on the participants' original definition of the problem. Do not feel confined by someone's definition. Secondly, always remember to help the other party "save face." No resolution is ultimately successful unless the subject can walk away with his or her sense of dignity preserved. You will find that the more you accomplish this goal, the less you will have to work for other solutions.

Chapter 8

Stalking and Predatory Behaviors In the Workplace

Up to this point, we have more often focused on violence that is generally *internal* to the organization (that is, perpetrated by the employee), with threats and/or behaviors in which there is a strong *affective* or emotional component, related to an identifiable source of stress. While there may be a range of stressors (including events external to the organization), there is generally an internal triggering event or central issue that has angered the subject. This emphasis is not without reason, as this is what represents most of the aggressive behavior that generally comes to our attention.

The workplace however, is not immune to violence and aggression of the more predatory type, when an individual is motivated by more sinister, goal-oriented, and egocentric motives. Individuals with chronically maladaptive social and personality disorders are more prevalent in this category, plus our concerns may be focused on aggressive behaviors that are more planned, purposeful, and prolonged in nature. Concerns about manipulation and deception may be more central, thereby complicating the work of the company's threat management team. The workplace is also not immune to violence that is perpetrated by someone from outside the organization, as previously discussed in relation to domestic issues.

I am not referring here to more random acts of violence that are committed by those who do not have a relationship with or who are not previously known to the organization, such as an act of violence committed during a robbery, for example. Our focus here represents a basic overview of predatory behavior that is directed toward members of the organization as part of a perceived relationship.

This chapter also includes a discussion on stalking, which is a particular (but not rare) set of behaviors. While stalking is often more driven by affective factors, it nevertheless involves some of the same focused and purposeful aspects of predatory behavior, such that effective management requires similar considerations.

The basic assessment and management model offered within this volume is not altered in these circumstances, but there are several elements that should be considered and emphasized when encountering these kinds of behaviors, as will be discussed. A team-oriented approach as previously described that carefully considers the ramifications of all decisions is even more critical in these instances.

Affective vs. Predatory Violence

As noted above, most of the aggression that we encounter in the workplace is *affective*, that is to say that there is a significant emotional and reactive component. *Predatory* violence, as defined here, is significantly different, in that it is generally more planned and purposeful, and less driven by primary emotional needs.

Any kind of labeling or categorization always runs the risk of over-simplifying and dichotomizing behavior that falls—more often than not—on a continuum. We often cannot completely separate acts of violence into either affective or predatory. What is most important for our purposes is the degree to which the behavior is predatory in nature, which will affect the way we manage the situation. Aggression that is primarily affective or emotionally driven may have certain predatory elements, and many incidents of primarily predatory violence may involve significant emotionality. For a more detailed description of the difference between these two categories, read Meloy's (2000) review of the subject. (See Bibliography for details.)

Affective violence generally refers to that which is accompanied by anger, fear, or any intense emotion or combination of emotions. Generally, the individuals who threaten or commit this kind of violence themselves feel threatened and are highly aroused. Their behavior is designed essentially to remove or reduce the threat that they are internally experiencing, and they are operating in a relatively defensive mode. Affective violence is usually time-limited and is generally temporarily connected to a perceived threat or object of concern. With individuals who are in the midst of committing this kind of aggressive act, we generally witness signs of increased autonomic arousal, in that their face may be flushed, they are heavily perspiring, their muscles are tensed, and so forth. We usually see these people coming. They present signs and symptoms that we can often identify before the violence occurs.

Predatory violence on the other hand, refers to generally planned or purposeful violence that is carried out with less emotion. The individual is generally focused on his or her target and may actually act long after a triggering event. The perpetrator is often thoughtful and deceptive and very focused on his or her goal—a goal that may be related to internal dynamics (i.e., delusions) that are not always obvious. These acts of violence may be carefully planned, to fulfill the subject's private agenda.

The Psychopathic Personality

When speaking of predatory violence, we often encounter what psychologists and psychiatrists refer to as "personality (or characterological) disorders," and more specifically, those disorders that reflect a disturbed capacity to develop and maintain relationships. Predominant in this category is the *antisocial personality disorder,* which is the diagnosis currently in use to cover the broad spectrum of antisocial behavior. This diagnostic category is primarily based on behavioral criteria and describes someone who engages in antisocial, aggressive, or otherwise irresponsible behaviors, with a reckless disregard for others and the rules of society.

Many of us are more familiar perhaps with the term "psychopath" or "sociopath," closely related terms that are historically used to define a constellation of personality characteristics—characteristics that create an image that is well-recognized and well-represented in the media.

These individuals are self-serving, manipulative, and suffer from a relative lack of empathy for others. Their ability to develop and maintain social relationships or any degree of loyalty is quite compromised. They often feel entitled and have a grandiose sense of self-worth. Their affect can be relatively shallow with a general lack of remorse or guilt for their actions. They can be impulsive and have difficulty delaying gratification and accepting responsibility for their actions. These individuals may be able to sustain appropriate behaviors in most circumstances, all hidden under a veil of deception, charm, and what appears to be self-confidence (but which actually extends to grandiosity).

Again, it is not the intent of the threat assessment process to diagnose or to determine if the subject is or is not a psychopath. The importance of noting the existence of this class of rather enduring personality characteristics is only important in terms of how it contributes to the assessment and the eventual management process. Many individuals may have psychopathic or related characteristics, and their personality may tend in that direction, but without meeting all of the criteria. Regardless, an individual who is relatively impulsive, who lacks the ability to form emotional attachments, and whose behavior suggests deception and manipulation will require an approach and a management system that needs to remain fully cognizant of those particular characteristics.

Any kind of risk management plan has to take into consideration the motivations of the subject and the subject's ability and willingness to control his or her actions within the established parameters. The difficulty of assessing and managing individuals with psychopathic characteristics is that they are by definition deceptive, manipulative, and—for lack of a better term—"sneaky." These individuals can be quite intelligent and so skilled in manipulation that they can (and do) "pass" many psychological evaluations without being discovered. Hence, as mentioned in previous chapters, the importance of having the assessment process conducted by professionals who have experience in working with this population.

Just as society contains a certain percentage of these individuals (anywhere from 1% to 4% are estimated to meet the full criteria for this diagnosis), that same percentage is likely to be found in the workplace, along with others who may fall at points further down that continuum. This is not a condition that is typically amenable to psychological treatment, and any management process has to be concerned with controlling and containing any security risks that would be anticipated and consistent with the assessment.

It should also be noted that there are other personality variables, besides those of the antisocial personality disorder, that involve problems with social *attachment*—that is, the ability to effectively bond with others. These will be encountered often in cases involving inappropriate social responses, such as stalking. These are varied and in their more maladaptive manifestations, they are represented by a range of clinical terms, such the *borderline personality disorder*, which often includes a history of unstable and intense relationships, with chronic feelings of abandonment. Other diagnostic categories may include the *narcissistic personality disorder*, who experience a grandiose sense of self-importance, the *schizoid personality disorder*, marked by extreme social detachment, and the *dependent personality disorder*, manifested by an excessive need for dependence.

The Impact of Paranoia and Delusional Thinking

Violence and threats of violence can occur as a direct or indirect result of an irrational belief system on the part of the subject. There are actually many psychological reasons why an individual may entertain irrational or delusional beliefs.

It is safe to say that we all, as human beings, maintain some assumptions that are not shared by everyone. We also may have certain philosophies or religious beliefs that are not always consistent with data, but are based rather on faith or assumptions that are not universally shared. We each interpret "reality" in our own manner. In our discourse among even good friends who are otherwise intelligent and sane, we will occasionally shake our heads in disbelief when we hear of another's political or religious belief that is (in our mind) beyond reason.

This qualification is presented as a reminder that irrational beliefs can be held by those who are otherwise normal and without significant psychopathology. We all have a tendency to selectively attend to that data which is consistent with our preconceived notions and selectively ignore (or explain away) that which does not. Human beings are driven to avoid "cognitive dissonance," that is, they have a need to ensure that their beliefs and experiences are not inconsistent with each other. If an event occurs that is contrary to the individual's belief system, then either the belief must change, or the event has to be interpreted differently. A degree of self-delusion occurs throughout our lives and can certainly surface under stress. Individuals under extreme stress can and do develop beliefs that may internally serve to help them maintain some kind of stability. A lover's refusal to believe that a cherished and central relationship has ended is a simple and common example.

Our concerns here are certainly not just with simply strongly held opinions that are simply unreasonable, but with those rather fixed set of beliefs that are compelling (or can compel) the individual toward actions that are inappropriate and potentially dangerous.

The development of paranoid and otherwise delusional

thought processes at a pathological level can occur as the result of a variety of psychological conditions. Major emotional disorders, such as a bipolar disorder, can frequently lead to psychosis, a state of disorganization that can include delusions and hallucinations. A bipolar disorder is a major emotional disorder that can include elements of extreme depression and/or mania. During either depressive or manic episodes, the individual can suffer from significant delusions and hallucinations. During a manic phase, this can become particularly challenging in risk management. The manic individual is highly energetic, agitated, and often engaged in self-destructive behaviors, oblivious to the consequences. This is fortunately a condition that frequently responds to appropriate treatment that generally includes medication. Getting the manic individual into treatment is the difficult part.

There are other disorders that can cause a psychotic state that are referred to as "cognitive" or "thought disorders." Included in this group is schizophrenia. Paranoid-based delusions are a frequent symptom, and in the severe phases, the individual can be completely disorganized and out of control. As with other major mental disorders, risk management cannot successfully be completed without getting this individual into treatment. Individuals who suffer from this condition may experience auditory hallucinations, often voices that sometimes issue commands. Violence can result if the individual feels compelled by the voices or if he or she delusionally assumes that a particular individual is responsible for these voices in some manner or somehow has a controlling influence.

Delusions can be the result of what is referred to as a "delusional disorder." This condition is quite significant and interesting when it occurs. The individual who is so diagnosed may appear quite "normal" and may indeed be functioning quite well in the community, without any apparent odd or unusual behaviors. However, he or she harbors a well-encapsulated belief or set of beliefs that are clearly delusional in nature and that are sometimes (but not always) bizarre. These delusions may be of a *persecutory type* (that they or someone to whom they are close are being chronically mistreated), a *jealous type* (i.e., imaging that their partner is unfaithful), or a *grandiose type* (that they enjoy a special position of inflated worth or power), among others. This also includes the *"erotomanic,"* which is described in the section under stalking, referring to those who are under the delusion that another person is in love with them.

This condition does occur in the workplace and can catch other employees off guard. It is a difficult condition to treat, and needless to say, the subject is not inclined to enter treatment or engage in any process that suggests that his or her beliefs are not real. It is equally stressful for the other employees, particularly the subject's friends, who have to cope with the dissonance produced by the revelation of this belief system.

It should be obvious how a delusional belief can prompt an aggressive act, especially if the subject believes that he or she is being attacked, persecuted, or mistreated in some way. The extent to which the delusions include an element of *paranoia* is a significant risk factor. An individual who is deeply distrustful and suspicious about the motives of others can be more apt to respond in a defensive and reactive manner to these perceived attacks.

A particular aspect of delusional thinking is what is referred to as "ideas of reference," in which the individual believes that certain events have some sort of special and personal meaning that is consistent with his or her belief system. These can be random events and completely unrelated in any manner to this individual. A common example is seen with those who stalk celebrities and those in the media, because of statements or actions that the stalker believes were specifically intended for him and for essentially no one else.

Paranoid delusions can occur as part of any of the above-mentioned psychological conditions. In addition, paranoia can represent a chronic aspect of an enduring personality system, which can include a lifetime of suspiciousness, distrust, and oversensitivity to perceived attacks. Individuals who are diagnosed as having a *paranoid personality disorder* are constantly "on guard" and can read demeaning or threatening meanings into even casual and innocent remarks. They doubt the loyalty of others and are quick to react angrily—anger being the emotional hallmark of these individuals. Further, they persistently bear grudges and do not forget (or forgive) perceived injustices.

When an individual who tends toward paranoia is under significant stress (stress that may be exacerbated by his or her paranoid beliefs), this individual may be quite reactive and emotionally vigilant. All of the features of these individuals' personality thus mentioned—their distrust, suspiciousness, and persecutory beliefs—are intensified, as they may become less rational. Their defensive nature may eventually take on a more offensive quality, and they may feel quite justified in their attacks.

Stalking Behaviors

The behavior that we refer to as "stalking" has always existed, but has only recently become more recognized and part of our everyday vocabulary, in part perhaps due to our present-day interest (read "obsession") with celebrities. Stalking has actually now become a crime in all 50 states, beginning with California's initiative in 1991, which was largely in response to the tragic result of a celebrity stalking case involving actress Rebecca Schaeffer.

While we frequently may think of stalking as something that only happens with highly visible celebrities or public figures, *most cases of stalking occur with ordinary citizens.* A 1997 report indicated that *8%* of adult American women and 2% of adult American men have been stalked sometime in their lives.[1] An estimated 1 million adult women and 400,000 adult men are stalked annually in the United States. These percentages can be equally applied to the workplace. As noted in a previous chapter, stalking as a consequence of domestic violence actually occurs quite frequently in the workplace.

There are many definitions of stalking, but most generally focus on a behavioral pattern of following or harassing another person, in which there is a credible threat to that person, or in a manner that evokes fear in the victim. Stalking involves a *pattern* of rather persistent and intrusive behavior that is unwanted by the victim. In most cases (but not all), the stalker is aware that the victim does not desire this behavior, and the act of stalking serves as a means of intimidating and/or controlling that individual.

The frequency of violence among stalkers toward their victims is reported to be anywhere from the 25% to 45% range, with violence from stalkers who have a history of prior sexual intimacies with their victims being much higher.[2] This is quite significant, as it represents a *very high* rate of violence when compared to other risk groups. Even without this relatively high rate of physical violence, stalking always, at the very least, represents a particular form of aggression: a prolonged (and sometimes recurring) set of actions that harass and intimidate their victims, who are often forced to live under a chronic level of distress and fear.

Stalking and the Workplace

Stalking in the workplace can take many forms and can occur for a variety of different reasons. It may involve one employee stalking another employee, or an employee may be a victim of stalking from someone outside the organization. There may have been an existing or previous relationship from which the victim cannot successfully disengage. It may involve a spouse or significant other who is not employed by the company, but who stalks his or her partner at the workplace because that is the only time that the stalker can successfully locate the victim.

Stalking can occur due to a delusional belief system, in which someone believes that he has a relationship with the victim—a belief that is not based in reality or shared by the victim. These delusions can be the result of a variety of psychological factors that can, in turn, be manifestations of various personality, cognitive, and/or emotional disorders. Finally, stalking can occur as a consequence of predatory behaviors that are related to significant antisocial personality characteristics.

Utilizing a typology established by Mike Zona and John Lane (1993), stalking can be classified into three categories, all of which can be experienced within the workplace:

1) The simple obsessional
2) The love obsessional
3) The erotomanic

The *"simple obsessional"* type of stalking occurs when the victim and the perpetrator have some kind of prior relationship which may or may not be intimate. One individual may be seeking to reunite with a spouse, lover, or ex-partner—or one partner may have an unrealistically high level of emotional investment, such that he or she is unable to separate, even from a relationship that may not have been considered that significant by the other party. Another manifestation may occur when an individual seeks to stalk or harass or terrorize someone because of a perceived slight or injustice, which may happen if an ex-employee stalks a supervisor, for example. This behavior generally occurs due to an overattachment to the victim and/or as a means of intimidating or harassing him or her.

The *"love obsessional"* type occurs when there is *not* an existing relationship between the victim and his or her perpetrator; however, the perpetrator *believes* that he or she is in love with the victim—and believes that the victim may even feel likewise if they would only give it consideration. This typically begins with a flurry of correspondence and attempts to contact the victim. At some point, the pursuer experiences disappointment and rejection, which can, in turn, lead to frustration, feelings of humiliation, and possibly anger. At this point, the pursuer's love may morph into a campaign of revenge. This involves significant fantasy, generally in someone with a history of social and/or psychological maladjustment. This is not restricted to celebrities, and can occur in any setting, with the behaviors emerging after a long period of fantasy, and sometimes without any real interaction with the victim.

The case of the *"erotomanic"* is relatively unusual, in that the perpetrator is under a delusional belief that the victim is in love with him or her. This is a rather unique and relatively less common situation, in which the majority of the perpetrators are female and the victims are often older men of a relatively higher socioeconomic status.

All of the above types of stalking can and do occur within most work environments, and represent a regular part of our caseload. The most prevalent is the "simple obsessional," whom most threat assessment professionals have to encounter on a relatively frequent basis. These can be the result of former intimacies, in which a partner is attempting to re-establish a relationship. It also includes situations in which there is an active campaign of revenge and/or harassment. As previously noted, a significant percentage of domestic violence finds itself in the workplace, and many organizations have to confront the angry and irrational spouse in the parking lot or the lobby (if they are lucky enough to stop him there).

The "love obsessional" type does occur in the workplace, but somewhat less frequently. We periodically encounter individuals, for example, who are somewhat socially maladjusted and suffer from a rather well-encapsulated internal delusional disorder, which sometimes extends to include a coworker within their fantasies. This actually may represent a longstanding condition in a relatively quiet or not otherwise interactive employee, whose condition was not obvious to anyone until the behaviors erupt, due to some kind of situational triggering event. This can involve an infatuation and a desire for intimacy with a coworker, or may involve aggressive behaviors toward someone who is believed to represent a threat.

More frequently, we see this kind of stalking behavior in work environments in which the employees are in front of a camera or are otherwise known to the public. In this era of 24-hour news, weather, and entertainment networks, when the potential object of affection appears on the screen with great regularity and frequency, this kind of remote "love obsessional" behavior appears to be on the increase. This can all be reinforced by the ability of the obsessed perpetrator to believe that he or she can communicate easily with the victim (i.e., through e-mail). All this is even further reinforced if the victim actually decides to respond to his correspondence.

While rare, the "erotomanic" is actually more prevalent than one would perhaps anticipate in certain environments. Chief executive officers, company presidents, and other leaders of certain high-profile corporations have actually become so well known that they can attract the same kind of attention generally experienced by those in the entertainment world. I have personally been involved in two cases just in the past six months, in which an erotomanic female in each case was obsessed with the president of a large corporation whom she had never met, but was under a strongly-held belief that this business leader was in love with her. Both of these stalkers were considered to be rational, normal citizens by those in their community, but internally maintained a strongly held delusional belief that was relatively impervious to any kind of reasoned discourse.

The impact of stalking on the victim is quite significant. Most suffer major disruptions in their lives. These kind of intrusive behaviors create so much imbalance, fear, and anxiety that victims typically suffer significant psychological effects, including post-traumatic stress disorder. The stalker's persistence (sometimes for years), the seemingly pervasive presence, the manipulative attempts to make contact, the fear that one's family will be at risk—all create an umbrella of fear and dread that leads to continuous vigilance. In many cases, the perpetrator's obsession is not amenable to any kind of intervention strategy, such that the primary goals become those of control and containment, often with the help of law enforcement and the courts.

Cyberstalking

The Internet has been a boom for stalking behaviors for a variety of reasons. First of all, it is easy. Individuals can now use the Internet to threaten, harass, or otherwise induce fear in target victims, in a manner that is much more difficult to trace.

It is a cheap and easy way to vent one's frustrations or to harass an individual, all with relatively little effort or planning. Further, the Internet provides this individual with a wealth of information about the victim, thereby increasing the means and ability to harass that individual.

The anonymity of the process actually widens the range of individuals who may utilize this vehicle, who otherwise may have been reluctant to do so, for fear of discovery. The individual does not feel as accountable and is less likely to feel constrained by any kind of laws—or even believe that this represents an intrusive behavior. It may embolden those who normally would not be confrontational in any other manner.

The nature of the Internet also facilitates the use of fantasy in individuals who may not have or cannot establish other social outlets. The relative lack of stimuli allows the individual to incorporate his or her fantasy into this relationship, developing an image of the other that is far from reality. This allows for an increase in misperceptions, more unrealistic expectations, and finally, a greater possibility for eventual feelings of disappointment and/or rejection.

As with all forms of threatening communications, e-mail threats are often delivered anonymously, which increases the complexity of risk assessment. It is often important in these cases to be very careful in any decision to respond, as we want to avoid initially stifling these communications. Oftentimes, the threat assessment professional requires as much data as possible in order to help identify the risk, the particular perpetrator and his or her motivations. In order to reduce the impact on the victim, a separate mailbox can be established in which mails from this individual can be diverted, in order to continue to collect data, monitor the communications, and assess the nature of any risk.

Management of Predatory and Stalking Behaviors

As noted earlier, the guiding principles of threat assessment and management do not change when considering cases involving these kinds of behaviors. However, the threat assessment team should be particularly cautious in these situations, as these are, by definition, the result of more goal-directed, sometimes sinister motives in individuals who may be quite focused, organized, and manipulative. As noted previously, the incidence of violence is relatively higher in cases involving stalking. Further, individuals with predatory intent are often more intelligent, deceptive, and manipulative, and less restrained by social expectations, emotions, or conscience. There may also be a delusional component that does not respond to reason, and the individual is one who often is quite adept and invested in the pursuit.

The Team Approach

First and foremost, this is an area where the *multi-disciplinary team* approach becomes most critical for success. These are often complex cases that require a multifaceted, long-term, and well-coordinated approach. It will require an understanding of the perpetrator's behavior such that professional *psychological assessment* is usually required. *Security* needs to be managed very carefully and with the full attention and involvement of those professionals who specialize in this area. *Legal consultation* is often required to address the company's obligations, and to identify available legal remedies. Managers and all critical company personnel who may have a chance to interact with this individual need to understand the assessment, the management plan, and their respective roles.

Utilizing External Resources

Resources external to the organization are often part of the "team" or at least have major role to play in these cases. These kinds of behaviors are generally not easily controlled without involving resources from the community. It often takes the proverbial village. Law enforcement, the criminal justice system, mental health, and other social service agencies are all potential partners in helping to contain and control these risks. Further, other members of the victim's (and sometimes the perpetrator's) community and family may also be instrumental in helping to monitor and/or control the risk in certain cases.

Communication and coordination among these groups is critical, to make certain that all are "on the same page." In many circumstances, the goals of law enforcement, for example, may not remain consistent with the goals of the victim or the company at each stage of the process, and each of the resources may have different interpretations of its respective role. Any active intervention such as involving law enforcement, obtaining court orders, initiating commitment proceedings, etc., should always be carefully considered in light of the potential long-range ramifications on the victim's safety. As with the medical profession, the team should first of all strive to "cause no harm."

The Victim's Role

Effective risk management requires that the team also stay in communication and work closely with the victim. The victim must understand what his or her obligations are in this process. Many victims will actually remain in contact with the stalker in an ill-advised effort to reduce their risk, but which may actually reinforce the perceived relationship or even inflame the individual. Having the victim contact the stalker will generally do nothing but reinforce his or her behavior and is rarely, if ever, advised.

While we do not want the victim to communicate with the stalker, some other lines of communication may need to be established to provide us with a way to monitor and provide valuable data about the perpetrator. As someone involved in both the assessment and management process, I generally would prefer that communications from the stalker not be completely stifled, at least in the early phases, as it provides critical data for the assessment and monitoring process.

The interview with the victim should be thorough enough to understand the existing relationship (if any) with the stalker, and all of the factors that may be influencing this type of behavior.

The victim needs to understand that his or her honesty is absolutely essential, as there may be some fact that the victim may find embarrassing and may fail to reveal. Risk assessment in these cases is, as always, a dynamic process that has to take into consideration the specific dynamics of that particular case and that particular relationship.

Victims must understand what their responsibility is for their own safety, and understand that the legal system, their employer, and other agencies are not able in most cases to absolutely guarantee anyone's safety. The victim must take personal responsibility, be actively involved in learning and engaging in risk-reducing behaviors, and be in constant communication with the company's threat response team. The victim must understand the importance of a cooperative team approach and of remaining consistent with the team's strategic decisions. This individual may require coaching by a security specialist or law enforcement professional in regard to how to best protect herself, establish routines, and set up environments to help reduce risk.

It is extremely important to document and maintain evidence of any kind of intrusive behaviors. Unfortunately, many victims will discard these unwanted letters and e-mails, but all are valuable in terms of monitoring the individual, assessing the risk, and documenting the evidence for any future legal action. This documentation may be critical in the case of future legal action, and is always helpful when analyzing patterns that may emerge.

The Role of Law Enforcement and Prosecution

Due to the high risks involved, appropriate security precautions are always advisable, along with any other actions that can help protect the victim. The use of law enforcement and the court system is often requisite in many of these cases. The threat manager will often need help with those individuals who are likely to ignore boundaries in a dangerous manner.

Any legal action, such as protective or restraining orders, should be carefully considered. Any kind of active intervention that involves law enforcement or approaching the individual should be analyzed and considered in terms of the potential benefits, along with the relative costs. In many of these cases, for example, the pursuer is often driven by feelings of humiliation, paranoia, and a belief that the victim and her allies have ruined his life. If an action is taken that reinforces and enhances these feelings (and therefore may increase risk to the victim), then the process needs to be carefully planned and considered, with the goals clearly defined and with the possible consequences fully anticipated. The individual's violation history, his mental status, and understanding the nature of his obsession will be instrumental in predicting how he may or may not respond to these kind of actions. The experience and commitment of the local law enforcement agency will be equally critical.

It is always advised that a relationship be developed with individual members of local law enforcement, and that they be involved at a level that facilitates their appreciation of the situation, the needs of the victim, and the nature of their role within the process. The same holds true for those situations when a decision is made to facilitate mental health commitment proceedings. It is imperative that someone in the assessment team is in communication with those medical personnel who are responsible for making decisions in the interest of public safety. They need to understand the history of the situation and what may be at stake.

The Role of Psychotherapy

Finding a way to encourage the subject into a mental health treatment program is often a goal in many of these cases, as many of these behaviors can be the result of cognitive, emotional, or personality disorders. Certainly, the threat management team may require the help and leverage of others, such as the courts, or even the subject's family, in order to help bring this about. Whereas mental health treatment by itself may not represent a solution, it can be an important ingredient, even in cases involving the relatively enduring personality disorders.

Whereas some conditions (or some individuals) may be relatively resistant to treatment, there can be often significant enough improvement to result in less overall risk. Medication, for example, may not completely eliminate the delusions of someone who suffers from a delusional disorder, but it can be of help in terms of his or her ability to control the delusions or function more appropriately, in spite of these delusions. Some medications such as the SRIs—generally utilized as an antidepressant—have been quite effective in helping their users bring obsessive thinking under better control. For many of the personality disorders, even the antisocial personality disorder, the appropriate treatment approach can, at the very least, help them learn to control their problematic behaviors (especially if there are other motivations, such as staying out of jail).

Finally, the involvement of a mental health professional can be a valuable asset to any threat management plan. Most medical and psychological professionals are well aware of their obligations to respond appropriately if they believe that their patient or client represents a risk to cause harm to someone else. The mental health practitioner can also serve as an advocate who can help the subject and his family identify other supportive resources, at different stages of the treatment process.

Preparing for the Long Term

In cases involving persistent predatory and/or obsessive behavior, there has to be an understanding among everyone involved that this may require a long-term effort. A long-range perspective should therefore be a guiding principle in the development of any kind of monitoring and management process. The team should identify critical points in the future that could serve to elevate the risks, and should be prepared to periodically monitor or assess the individual if the psychological assessment suggests that this is warranted. Stalking, in particular, is driven by an obsession that can last for years, and that does not disappear just because the individual is sent to jail, for example. Any management plan has to anticipate those future moments when the risks may again rise: when the perpetrator is released from jail, if he stops taking his medication, if some of the resources put into place cease to be effective, and so forth. This is the time when the ball is most often dropped, with tragic consequences.

In conclusion, the workplace is not immune to antisocial, predatory, or dangerously obsessive behaviors. This is a much more prevalent part of our culture than is generally realized, and can literally happen to anyone. In my experience, the introduction of "cyberstalking" has led to an increase of stalking-related behaviors and a belief that there is a greater degree of anonymity. In the cases involving domestic violence, employees should come to understand—through the company's workplace violence training programs—that any stalking or revenge-related behaviors directed toward the employee should be responsibly reported, as it may affect everyone's safety. These are all cases that require a coordinated, comprehensive approach. Having a pre-existing relationship with critical community resources, such as law enforcement and mental health programs, always represents an important measure of prevention.

Endnotes

[1] P. Tjaden & N. Thoennes (1997), as cited in Meloy (1998).
[2] R. Meloy, *The Psychology of Stalking.* (San Diego: Academic Press, 1998).

Epilogue

The Future
(if we want it)

Violence—and aggressive behavior in the workplace in particular—has become a reality of our time. However, there are other realities that receive far less attention.

I am referring here to the progress that has been made, and is still being made, in the study and understanding of the causes and development of conflict and aggression. I have been involved professionally in enough of these incidents to know that we, individually and collectively, have the resources to address and resolve these issues that lead to violence, and we can prevent the occurrence of the harmful consequences. However, most of what we know is of diminishing value if we choose to simply wait for a crisis to reach a certain level of severity, such that it literally forces a response.

Most of our institutions, including our judicial systems, have not elected to incorporate even a small portion of what we know in this area in any kind of proactive manner. Further, our reactive approaches often actually serve to aggravate the problems and even increase the risk. It is certainly an old story: prevention and early preparation rarely receive the attention that follows in the wake of a crisis.

Our society (American society in particular) sometimes appears fascinated by violence and all too willing to accept the consequences as a central part of the human condition. Further, we are so accustomed to it (and so afraid of it) that our traditional response is to turn our heads away and hope for the best. It is part of our folklore that there will always be gunfighters in the streets, and that all the rest of us can do is to just keep our heads down.

I do not intend in any way to paint an overly rosy picture of human nature. I know, and we all know, that violence has historically been part and parcel of the human experience, and I see nothing on the horizon to suggest that this will change in any significant manner. Aggressive behavior has to be accepted at a certain level. However, I do believe that we now have enough of an understanding of both how this behavior develops and how to effectively intervene in this process, such that we have the means to substantially reduce the development, escalation, and harmful effects of these acts of violence.

To some degree, our society and its institutions will first have to decide that it is indeed willing to surrender the assumptions presented above before any effective change can truly occur. As horrified as we are by these media events of workplace violence, we remain also somewhat accepting of it—and even fascinated to some degree. It is my opinion that we are still quite invested in the myth of the Wild West, as a defining cultural theme (a theme that still continues in today's cinema, albeit in other, less Western settings.)

All of that philosophical speculation aside, I have attempted in this volume to emphasize the importance of increasing our awareness of, and sensitivity to, those factors that are critical to the developing process that results in violent behavior. Many times, this awareness alone will effectively suggest the necessary steps to prevent the more dire consequences. However, we also have at our disposal a much better understanding of how to effectively intervene—and to even resolve the underlying issues.

Corporate managers often cannot always accomplish this by themselves. If the appropriate prevention program is in place, these events will often come to the attention of managers in time to resolve them successfully, bring in the appropriate resources, and avoid anyone getting hurt. An effective prevention program will generally reduce the possibility that the company will have to rely on its crisis response plan or outside intervention. However, just as the company may occasionally need help from contracted accountants and attorneys to make sense of tax and legal issues, specialists are sometimes similarly required in these potentially high-risk situations.

Finally, we have attempted to discuss in this volume the common mistakes that are made in this process. Most of them, as noted, have to do with denial and avoidance. Part of this may include the attempt (or at least the desire) to find an easily implemented "cookbook" that can provide standardized, approved responses that will make these issues disappear. I hope that I have been able to express throughout this book that both the complexity of human behavior and the stakes involved do not yet allow this. A thorough assessment process that examines and carefully considers the psychological, social, and situational particulars of each case cannot be short-circuited. Any resolution process of a situation that has risen to a level such that people are afraid for their lives must be sensitive to the particular variables that are critical to that situation. Without this, the creative solutions that are generally required to truly resolve the issue (and ensure long-term safety) will not be discovered.

We are truly living in an exciting time, in terms of our understanding and appreciation of the dynamics and development of aggressive behavior. The implementation of what we have learned represents another matter. If we want it, our organizational systems and social structures can institute procedures that can incorporate, utilize, and easily access this information when needed. We do not have to feel so vulnerable.

Appendix A

A Sample
Workplace Violence Policy

The Company is concerned about the increased incidence of workplace violence in our society and has therefore taken steps to help prevent incidents of violence from occurring in our place of employment. This Company is very concerned about the personal safety of both its employees and anyone doing business with this Company.

The Company therefore expressly prohibits any acts or threats of violence, whether expressed or implied, by any current or former employee against another employee in or outside the workplace at any time. The Company also will not tolerate any acts or threats of violence against customers, vendors, or any others who are engaged in business with or on behalf of the Company, whether at or away from the Company. Further, *any* conduct that creates an intimidating, hostile, offensive, or threatening work environment through unwelcome words, actions, or physical contact will not be tolerated.

All reports of incidents of this nature will be taken seriously and will be addressed promptly and appropriately. An employee who violates this policy will be subject to disciplinary action up to and including discharge and/or criminal penalties, and may be excluded from the premises.

Definition of Workplace Violence

Workplace violence is defined here as any conduct that is offensive or intimidating enough to result in another individual becoming reasonably fearful for his or her personal safety, or for the safety of their family or property. This pertains to behavior that occurs on Company premises, regardless of the relationship between the Company and the perpetrator or the victim of the behavior. It also includes acts that occur off Company premises, where the perpetrator is an employee or acting as a representative of the Company at the time, where the victim is an employee who is exposed to this conduct because of his or her work for the Company, or where there is a reasonable basis to believe that violence may occur against the target employee or others in the workplace.

Employee Responsibility

Employees are a necessary part of this policy. Any employee who becomes aware of a display of aggressive, abusive, or threatening behavior, or a threat or tendency to engage in such behavior by another employee, is to report such behavior to his immediate supervisor, to Security personnel, to Human Resources or to the Company's confidential Hotline (#). To the extent possible, such reports will be handled confidentially.

Employees have a further obligation to inform their immediate supervisor or Human Resources of any activity in the workplace involving current or former employees, customers, visitors, vendors, or other people that they believe could result in violence. This includes, for example, threats of violence, intimidating or confrontational behavior, and threatening or hostile comments. Employees should also report violence or threats of violence between employees that occur away from the work site.

Employee reports made pursuant to this policy will be dealt with in a confidential manner to the extent possible. The Company will not tolerate any form of retaliation against any employee for making a report under this policy. Likewise, no employee will suffer any retaliation from having complied with this policy.

Management Responsibility

It is the management's duty to demonstrate the Company's commitment to prohibiting and preventing violence in the workplace through training and increased awareness.

Management is responsible for taking action against threats, or acts of violence, toward employees committed by Company personnel, customers, outside vendors, family members, or others. All workplace violence referrals will be given priority attention and treated as serious violations of Company policy.

If members of Company management become aware of any violation, behavior, or perceived threat that may violate this policy, they are responsible for:

- Conducting an immediate preliminary inquiry
- Responding in a prompt and discreet manner
- Notifying Human Resource directors and those responsible for workplace violence oversight
- Thoroughly investigating the referral to establish all relevant facts and accountabilities
- Providing accurate documentation on all reported incidents as well as actions performed
- Identifying, with the help of division HR and Security, and communicating avenues of support for employees who may have expressed workplace violence concerns
- Evaluating the work environment in respect to the occurrence of workplace violence and making recommendations to prevent future incidents.

Weapons in the Workplace

The Company strictly prohibits employees from possessing weapons of <u>any</u> kind at the workplace. This prohibition explicitly includes firearms of any type, including those for which the holder has a legal permit. Other examples may include, but are not limited to, knives, mace, or any instrument or device used for an attack.

Employees are not permitted to bring weapons into the worksite, keep weapons on Company property, or have weapons in their personal vehicle while they are parked on the premises. The Company property covered by this policy includes property of any nature owned, controlled, or used by the Company including, but not limited to, parking lots, vehicles, offices, file cabinets, desks, and lockers. A violation of this may result in disciplinary action up to and including immediate discharge.

If the Company suspects that an employee may have violated this policy, the Company may request the employee to submit to a search of his or her person, personal effects, and vehicles. The Company may conduct searches of any Company property including, but not limited to, desks, lockers, file cabinets, computers, voicemail, Company vehicles, and any other property or equipment owned by the Company, at any time, without notice to or permission from affected employees. If an individual is asked to submit to a search and refuses, that individual will be considered insubordinate and will be subject to discipline up to and including discharge. Any weapons or evidence of violation of this policy will be confiscated, and may be turned over to law enforcement, as appropriate. Any illegal activity discovered during an inspection is subject to referral to the appropriate law enforcement authorities.

Response to a Serious Threat or Violent Act

The appropriate response for all types of workplace violence will vary. In most situations, the guidelines set forth above for employees and managers will apply. However, when confronted with an imminent threat of workplace violence, police authorities should be notified immediately by dialing 911. Employees in danger should be given the opportunity to leave the work environment for a safer location. Nothing in this policy is intended to prevent quick action to stop or reduce the risk of harm to anyone, including requesting immediate assistance from law enforcement or emergency response resources.

What to Expect from the Company

All incidents of violence or threats of violence that are reported will be taken seriously and investigated. The Company will decide whether its workplace violence policy has been violated, and whether preventative or corrective action is appropriate. The Company may consult with law enforcement authorities or other resources, as it deems appropriate, and may require examinations or other professional assessments through providers chosen by the Company to determine whether a perpetrator presents a threat to himself or others in the workplace. If a violation of this policy occurs, the Company will take appropriate preventative and corrective action, up to and including termination.

Guidelines for Prevention

Acts of violence cannot always be prevented or predicted with absolute certainty. However, threats or acts of aggression often escalate to a level of violence despite the fact that there were adequate warning signs that were not attended to or reported appropriately. All business units and respective managers should be aware of basic guidelines for workplace violence prevention and should conduct employee awareness and training programs as appropriate.

The purpose of this policy is preventive, not punitive. It is the responsibility of each and every employee to contribute to a safe working environment. The Company is committed to ensuring the personal safety of its employees and cannot do its part without the full cooperation of all employees.

Appendix B

An Organizational Self-Assessment Questionnaire

Yes   No

Pre-employment Screening

1. Does your company adequately check references with attention to any details regarding the employee's ability to get along with coworkers? _____ _____

2. Does your company carefully review the employee's application to uncover inconsistencies, significant gaps in employment and/or possible deception? _____ _____

3. In the pre-employment interview, is the applicant specifically asked about his or her ability to handle conflict and any other interpersonal issue that may be job-related?   _____ _____

4. Does the company's pre-employment screening include thorough criminal background checks?   _____ _____

Workplace Violence Policy

1. Does your company have a policy that clearly states the company's commitment to the issue of aggression and violence in the workplace?   _____ _____

2. Does this workplace violence policy clearly describe the broad range of aggressive behaviors that are not tolerated within the work environment?   _____ _____

3. Does the workplace violence policy specify what is expected of both the general employees and managers not only in terms of their own behavior but what they should do if and when they encounter behaviors of concern?   _____ _____

4. Does the policy explicitly detail the reporting process if an employee does have concerns about a potential risk?   _____ _____

Employee Awareness

1. Do you believe that your company has effectively communicated to all employees the importance of participation in the company's workplace violence program?   _____ _____

2. Do your employees understand the importance of being aware of and appropriately reporting potential warning signs?   _____ _____

Employee Training

1. Is there a training program in place that is regularly provided to the employees, that focuses on the company's workplace violence policy?   _____ _____

2. Is there a regular training program for supervisors that trains supervisors in regards to their specific responsibilities under the company's workplace violence policy?   _____ _____

3. Is there a regular training program for Human Resource, Corporate Security, and other managers who would be involved in decision-making in situations involving workplace violence?   _____ _____

Threat Response Planning

1. Does the company have a threat response team that is designated as primarily responsible for developing and maintaining the company's threat response plan? _____ _____

2. Does the company have a threat response plan that can guide critical personnel in situations involving threats of violence? _____ _____

Grievance, Disciplinary, and Termination

1. Do you believe that your company has an adequate process that addresses the grievances of employees who feel chronically mistreated? _____ _____

2. Do you believe that discipline is fairly and consistently applied within the organization? _____ _____

3. Do you believe that there are certain employees, because of their intimidating behavior, who are able to avoid disciplinary action? _____ _____

4. Do you believe that your company gives adequate consideration when at-risk employees are terminated or encounter any kind of adverse employee action? _____ _____

5. Are high-risk terminations conducted in a secure setting with attention to relevant security concerns?   _____ _____

6. Is the exit strategy for terminating employees conducted with concern for security and the employee's dignity?   _____ _____

Employee Assistance Programs

1. Does the company utilize any services that can help employees during times of stress?   _____ _____

2. Are the employees made adequately aware of these resources?   _____ _____

3. Do the employees utilize these resources or are they suspicious of its intent?   _____ _____

Outside Resources

1. Does the company consider utilizing outplacement services for terminated employees who may have difficulty finding employment?   _____ _____

2. Does the company have a good relationship with its local law enforcement agency?   _____ _____

3. Does the company have knowledge of a threat assessment professional who can aid the company when confronted by a potential threat of violence?   _____ _____

4. Is the company aware of its legal resources?   _____ _____

5. If the company does not have an internal security staff, is the company aware of a security consultant who could be called in when needed?   _____ _____

Supervisory and Conflict Resolution Skills Training

1. Does the company train supervisors in appropriate management and conflict resolution skills?   _____ _____

2. Is there any kind of program available that can help employees resolve conflict and help supervisors resolve conflict among their supervisees?   _____ _____

Physical Security

1. Has there been an assessment of physical security systems?   _____ _____

2. Can the company communicate to the employees quickly after a critical incident in order to either warn or address their concerns?   _____ _____

3. Is the company comfortable with its exposure to outside risks?   _____ _____

4. Is there adequate control of the access points into the physical work environment?   _____ _____

5. If necessary, is there a way to review any threatening correspondence from customers or other outside individuals?   _____ _____

6. How comfortable are you with the qualifications of the security firm that the company utilizes?   _____ _____

Cultural and Other Issues

1. Do the company's employees believe that they will be treated fairly, with respect, and in a confidential manner?   _____ _____

2. Is it generally considered acceptable for employees to approach either HR or the Employee Assistance Program for help when needed?   _____ _____

3. Is performance regularly reviewed in a direct, supportive and constructive manner?   _____ _____

4. Are the supervisors trained to recognize
    and deal very directly and quickly with
    any performance-related problems?   _____ _____

5. Does the company offer any kind of
    educational programs regarding stress
    management, harassment, and other
    issues that would promote health and   _____ _____
    safety?

6. Does the company have a plan for
    communicating with media should there
    be a critical incident at the company?   _____ _____

Appendix C

Violence Assessment: Interview Checklist

(attach additional pages if necessary)

Name of Subject: _____

Location: _____

Name of Person Completing Form: _____

I. Employment History

    1, Is the subject an employee? yes _____ no _____
       If so, how long have they been employed and what is their
       current position?

       _____

       _____

       _____

2. If the subject is not an employee, what is the subject's relationship to the company? _____

_____

_____

II. Workplace Behavior

1. Disciplinary History? yes _____ no _____
   Explain: _____

   _____

   _____

2. History of supervisory problems? yes _____ no _____
   Explain: _____

   _____

   _____

3. Current workplace grievances/issues? yes _____ no _____
   Explain: _____

   _____

   _____

4. History of threats? yes _____ no _____
   Explain: _____

   _____

   _____

5. History of conflict with coworkers? yes _____ no _____
   Explain: _____

   _____

   _____

6. Performance problems? yes _____ no _____
   Explain: _____

   _____

   _____

7. History of intimidating or aggressive behavior in the workplace?

yes _____ no _____

Explain: _____

_____

_____

8. Does the employee have friends in the workplace?

yes _____ no _____

Explain: _____

_____

_____

9. History of absences and/or tardiness? yes _____ no _____

Explain: _____

_____

_____

10. Are there individuals within the workplace that the subject has specifically targeted in any manner? yes ____ no ____

Explain: _____

_____

_____

11. Are there those in the workplace who are worried or afraid of the subject? yes _____ no _____

Explain: _____

_____

_____

12. When the subject is eating lunch or otherwise engaging in break activity at the workplace, is he or she usually alone or in a group with others?

Explain: _____

_____

_____

13. Would the subject be described as "full of himself" in that he is egotistical and has a rather high opinion of himself when compared to others? yes _____ no _____
Explain: _____

_____

_____

14. When confronted, does the subject take responsibility or tend to blame others?
Explain: _____

_____

_____

15. Are there significant variations in their energy level (from appearing sluggish and bored one day to being very excitable and anxious the next)? yes _____ no _____
Explain: _____

_____

_____

16. Is there a history of tantrum behavior that would include flying into fits of rage inappropriately and without warning?
yes _____ no _____
Explain: _____

_____

_____

17. Has the subject ever exhibited any aggressive behavior toward others in the workplace in any manner whatsoever?
yes _____ no _____
Explain: _____

_____

_____

18. Are people in the workplace afraid of approaching him or her? yes _____ no _____
Explain: _____

_____

_____

III. Relevant medical history:

1. Any knowledge of a potentially significant medical condition? yes _____ no _____
Explain: _____

_____

_____

2. Any knowledge of current use of prescriptions or other medication? yes _____ no _____
Explain: _____

_____

_____

3. Any knowledge of any kind of condition that could affect mental status, thinking, etc.? yes _____ no _____
Explain: _____

_____

_____

4. Any health problems within his or her family that could cause additional stress? yes _____ no _____
Explain: _____

_____

_____

5. Any history of significant head trauma or any other condition that could affect mental functioning? yes _____ no _____
Explain: _____
_____
_____

IV. Mental Status

1. Does the subject appear to have relative difficulty comprehending or understanding concepts in any relevant manner? yes _____ no _____
Explain: _____
_____
_____

2. Is he or she making bizarre statements or otherwise appearing to be out of touch with reality? yes _____ no _____
Explain: _____
_____
_____

3. Is the subject having difficulty with concentration and/or attention? yes _____ no _____
Explain: _____
_____
_____

4. Does he or she appear to be obsessed with certain individuals or certain subjects? yes _____ no _____
Explain: _____
_____
_____

5. Is there a history of suicidal thoughts or attempts?
   yes _____ no _____
   Explain: _____

   _____

   _____

6. Is there any knowledge that this individual has undergone treatment for a mental illness? yes _____ no _____
   Explain: _____

   _____

   _____

7. Is there any known or suspected history of drug and/or alcohol abuse? yes _____ no _____
   Explain: _____

   _____

   _____

8. Have there been any recent changes in self-care, hygiene, dress, etc.? yes _____ no _____
   Explain: _____

   _____

   _____

9. Have there been any recent changes in the subject's personality? yes _____ no _____
   Explain: _____

   _____

   _____

10. Is this individual considered by others to be very impulsive, to act without thinking, or to otherwise use poor judgment?
    yes _____ no _____
    Explain: _____

    _____

    _____

11. Is the employee overly obsessed with his or her job to the point that they appear to have no other interests?
yes _____ no _____
Explain: _____
_____
_____

V. Social/Family Life

1. Does the subject live with his or her family?
yes _____ no _____

_____
_____
_____

2. What is the known family history of the individual?
Explain: _____
_____
_____

3. Does the subject have friends within or outside the workplace? yes _____ no _____
Explain: _____
_____
_____

4. Does the subject have any particular hobbies or interests outside the workplace? yes _____ no _____
Explain: _____
_____
_____

5. Any knowledge of a history of domestic violence or sexual abuse? yes _____ no _____
Explain: _____
_____

6. Is there any indication of a history of violence within his or her family (parent, siblings, etc.)? yes _____ no _____
Explain: _____
_____
_____

7. How has the employee dealt with confrontation in the past?

_____
_____
_____

VI. Weaponry

1. Is there any knowledge of the subject's owning, possessing, or using weapons of any nature? yes _____ no _____
Explain: _____
_____
_____

2. Is there any knowledge of the individual exhibiting an increased fascination with weapons and/or violence?
yes _____ no _____
Explain: _____
_____
_____

VII. Other Issues

1. Is there any knowledge that the subject has had significant legal problems? yes _____ no _____
Explain: _____
_____
_____

2. Is there any known history of protective or restraining orders, imprisonment, or probation? yes _____ no _____
   Explain: _____
   _____
   _____

3. Is there any knowledge that the subject has exhibited aggressive behavior at any time in his or her past?
   yes _____ no _____
   Explain: _____
   _____
   _____

4. Is there any knowledge that the subject has current financial problems or has had financial problems in the past?
   yes _____ no _____
   Explain: _____
   _____
   _____

5. Is there any knowledge that the subject is undergoing a significant amount of stress currently? yes ____ no _____
   Explain: _____
   _____
   _____

6. Any recent losses or traumas that may be significant?
   yes _____ no _____
   Explain: _____
   _____
   _____

7. Has the subject ever mentioned that he belonged to a particular organization, club, or association, or would like to join one? yes _____ no _____
   Explain: _____
   _____
   _____

8. Has the subject, according to anyone's knowledge, engaged in any unusual sexual practices, harassment, or any kind of predatory or stalking behavior toward others within or outside the workplace? yes _____ no _____
   Explain: _____
   _____
   _____

9. Has the subject ever discussed suicide or made references to his or her death? yes _____ no _____
   Explain: _____
   _____
   _____

10. Has the subject ever made fatalistic comments such as "It really doesn't matter," "I have nothing to live for," etc.
    yes _____ no _____
    Explain: _____
    _____
    _____

11. Does the subject ever talk about his or her future in any manner? yes _____ no _____
    Explain: _____
    _____
    _____

12. Are there any concerns that the subject is not responsible or may be manipulative or deceitful with others?
    yes _____ no _____

Explain: _____

_____

_____

13. Is there anything else that is considered to be significant
    about this particular individual that causes concern?
    yes _____ no _____
    Explain: _____

    _____

    _____

    _____

    _____

    _____

Appendix D

A Sample
Return to Work Agreement

<u>AGREEMENT OF COMMITMENT</u>

In accordance with previous agreements, you have been on active employment and pay status but not actively working, pending your clearance to return to work by an independent evaluator, and after consultation with the Company's consultant and with your own treating physician.

The Company welcomes you back and looks forward to your return to work. We wish to make your transition a smooth and successful one. Listed below are the specific terms and conditions that pertain to your return to active work and continued employment. By signing this document, you understand and voluntarily agree that your continued employment is based on the following terms:

- You agree to continue in treatment as previously recommended by an independent evaluation and your own treating physician, which will include continued counseling, and involvement in both an anger management program and a substance abuse aftercare program, as has been recommended.

- You agree to release your treatment provider to discuss with the Company's threat assessment consultant the following issues:
  - Treatment compliance.
  - Any associated risks to the Company or its employees.
- You agree to submit to drug tests (blood tests or urinalysis) at any time required by the company during the 24 months following the signing of this agreement. You understand that if you refuse to take the drug test or if the test is positive, your employment will be terminated immediately.
- You understand that your previous job performance warrants close supervision for an extended period of time upon your return to work, and you will accept such supervision as a constructive part of your recovery.
- Any threats, threatening statements, intimidation, fights, harassment, or violent acts toward anyone associated with the company will result in immediate termination of employment.
- Consistent with company policy, management retains the right to search your locker without prior notification. You will also agree to allow management the right to search your personal vehicle without prior notification.
- Upon your return to work, you are to meet initially with your Human Resource Manager. You will continue to meet on a regular basis with that Human Resource Manager during an agreed-upon transition period, in order to discuss your progress and to review any concerns that you might have regarding your reintroduction to work. Please feel free to discuss with this representative any concerns or problems which may arise regarding these and other issues.
- You acknowledge that failure to comply with the terms listed herein could result in immediate termination of employment from the company.

- The contents of this document are to remain confidential. You are not to disclose the contents of this agreement to anyone outside of your treatment providers, with the exception of your designated union representative or attorney.

By signing this document, you are acknowledging that you understand the terms of this agreement and that you understand that continued employment with this company is contingent on meeting satisfactorily all the above items, and that your failure to do so may subject you to termination of employment.

_____   _____
Employee Signature   Date

_____   _____
Company Representative   Date

Appendix E

A Sample
Termination Agreement

CONFIDENTIAL SEPARATION AGREEMENT

The following is an agreement by and between _____
_____, "Employee" and _____,
"Company."

WHEREAS in light of recent circumstances, the Employee
and the Company believe that it is in the mutual best interest
to end the Employee's employment with the Company. This
separation agreement is made and entered into by the Employee
and the Company in order to reach an amicable termination
of their employment relationship and to promote harmonious
relations in the future.

Therefore, in consideration of the mutual promises contained in
this agreement, the sufficiency of which is hereby acknowledged,
the Employee and the Company do hereby agree as follows:

TERMINATION. The Employee agrees that his/her
employment with the Company will terminate effective _____
_____. Thereafter, accepted under otherwise what

is provided herein, no future compensation or benefits will accrue in his/her favor.

SEPARATION BENEFITS.

1. The Company agrees that upon the execution of this separation agreement, the Company will pay the Employee a severance allowance at the rate of _____ _____, subject to applicable taxes per month for the period beginning _____ and ending _____ .
2. The Company further agrees that upon the execution of this separation agreement, it will voluntarily permit the Employee to continue to participate through _____ _____, in the health or welfare plans, which the Company may, from time to time make available to its Employees, generally, to the extent that the Employee participated therein at the date of his/her termination.
3. The Company agrees that it will provide the Employee with career outplacement services throughout the term of this agreement.
4. The Company will not contest any application that the Employee may make for unemployment insurance compensation.

OBLIGATIONS OF EMPLOYEE. As consideration for the benefits provided by the Company to the Employee in this agreement, the Employee agrees to the following terms:

1. He/she, directly or by a family member or associate, is no longer to come within 500 yards of the Company property.
2. He/she, directly or by a family member or associate, is not to contact the Company or any of its Employees. Any communication should be directed through the Human Resources Manager named herein (_____ _____) and the Company's previously designated consultant who is acting in the company's behalf (_____ _____).

3. The Employee is to remain in contact with the Company's consultant, notifying him of any change in home address or telephone number.
4. In order to receive these extended health insurance benefits, the Employee must agree to continue in a counseling program through the EAP Services to help him with this transition, as has been previously recommended.
5. The Employee is to permit his counselor to release information to the Company's consultant as to the following issues:
   a. That you are attending and complying with counseling as recommended.
   b. That you are not at risk of harming yourself or others.
   c. That your current treatment procedures remain sufficient.
6. If the Employee is found not to be compliant with any of these obligations, as reported by the Company's consultant, then the Company is no longer obligated to continue providing the separation pay and benefits as previously noted.

RELEASE. In consideration for the above separation pay and separation benefits, the Employee agrees to release the Company and each of its directors, employees, agents, subsidiaries, affiliates, successors, and assigns from any and all charges, complaints, claims, liabilities, actions, causes of action, suits, demands, cost, losses, damages and expenses, of any nature whatsoever, known or unknown, including, but in no way limited to any claim arising out of their employment relationship or the termination of their employment relationship, which the Employee now has, owned or holds, or claims to have, owned or hold, on which the Employee at any time has claimed to have, owned or hold against them.

CONFIDENTIALITY. The Employee, his/her spouse and the Company, their attorneys, agents and employees, all agree to keep completely confidential the amount, terms, facts, and circumstances given arise to this agreement, and will not disclose, directly or indirectly, any such information to any person or entity (including, but not limited to, past, present, or future employees of the Company) with the following exceptions:

The Employee may disclose the information regarding this agreement to:

- His/her healthcare provider.
- A professional tax advisor or tax return preparer for the limited purpose of obtaining advice regarding or preparing such tax return or returns as may be necessary.
- Any and all relevant taxing authorities. The Company may send a letter to disclose such information as is necessary for a legitimate business purpose.

DISCLAIMER OF LIABILITY. The Employee recognizes and acknowledges that the fulfillment by the Company of its obligations under this agreement should not be construed as an admission of any acts or wrongdoing whatsoever by the Company against the Employee or any other person and the above-mentioned obligations are agreed to in order to resolve the circumstances which caused the agreement to be entered into.

FULL KNOWLEDGE AND VOLITION. The Employee represents and acknowledges that, prior to execution of this agreement, he/she has been advised to discuss all aspects of this agreement with an attorney, that he/she has been provided a reasonable and sufficient period of time within which to consider this agreement, he/she has carefully read and understands all the provisions of this agreement, and that he/she is voluntarily entering into this agreement. The Employee acknowledges and confirms that the only consideration for signing this agreement is the terms and conditions stated in this agreement, that no other promise or agreement of any kind, except those set forth in this agreement, have been made to him/her by any person to cause him/her to sign this agreement.

By: _____   _____
Employee   Date

By: _____   _____
Company Representative   Date

References

Bliss, W. *Legal, Effective References* Alexandria, VA: Society for Human Resource Management, 2001.

Clay, R. "Securing the Workplace: Are Our Fears Misplaced?" *Monitor on Psychology*, 31 (2000): 9.

Corcoran, M. & J. Cawood. *Violence Assessment and Intervention.* New York: CRC Press, 2003.

Covey, S. *The 7 Habits of Highly Effective People.* New York: Simon & Schuster, 1989.

DeBecker, G. *The Gift of Fear.* Boston: Little, Brown & Co., 1997.

Fisher, R. & W. Ury. *Getting to Yes.* New York: Penguin Books, 1991.

Ford & Harrison, LLP (2002). Unpublished material.

Labig, C.E. *Preventing Violence in the Workplace.* New York: American Management Association, 1995.

Leather, P., ed. *Work-related Violence: Assessment and Intervention.* London: Routledge, 1999.

Meloy, J. R., ed. *The Psychology of Stalking.* San Diego: Academic Press, 1998.

Meloy, J. R. *Violence Risk and Threat Assessment.* San Diego: Specialized Training Services, 2000.

Stone, A.V. *Fitness for Duty: Principles, Methods and Legal Issues.* New York: CRC Press, 2000.

Turner, J. & M. Gelles. *Threat Assessment: A Risk Management Approach.* New York: Haworth Press, 2003.

Ury, W. *Getting Past No.* New York: Bantam Books, 1993.

Zona, M., K. Sharma & J. Lane. "A Comparative Study of Erotomanic and Obsessional Subjects in a Forensic Sample." *Journal of Forensic Sciences, 38* (4) (1993), 894-903.